A China Story:

From Peip'ing
to Beijing

James B. Hendry

ISBN: 1493638041
ISBN-13: 9781493638048
Library of Congress Control Number: 2013920642
CreateSpace Independent Publishing Platform,
North Charleston, SC

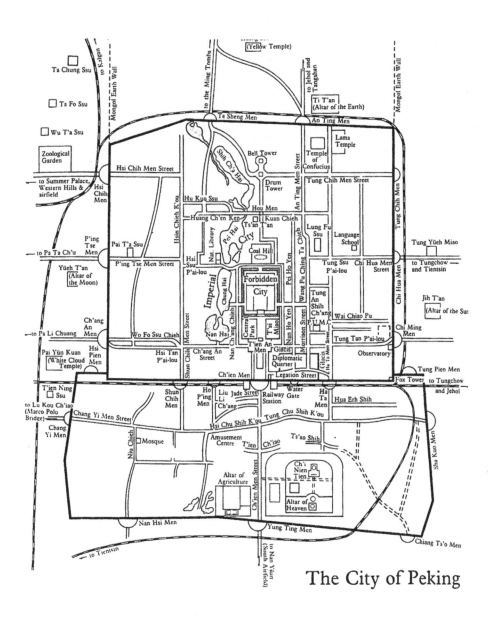

The City of Peking

For Lyn, no longer among us, but always in our hearts.

On the occasion of Lyn's retirement from Walt Whitman High School in Bethesda, Maryland, the students in her Far East History class presented her with a framed copy of a poem by an esteemed Chinese poet, Po Chu-Yi. The subject of the poem is a classical painter of bamboo, Master Hsiao, who is aging and no longer able to paint the master works for which he is famed. By linking the accomplishments of these two people, Master Hsiao and Lyn, the students found a profoundly moving and tasteful way to express their high regard for Lyn as a teacher.

Painting Bamboo: A Song

Of all the plants, bamboo is the most difficult to paint;
Among ancient and modern painters, none has caught its likeness.
Master Hsiao's brush alone brings out the similitude —
He's the one supreme artist in the history of painting.
Others paint the bamboo thick and gnarled;
Hsiao paints each spear lean and sturdy.
Others paint the bamboo tufts lifeless, limp and drooping.
Hsiao paints the branches alive, as if each leaf were seen to move.
Without roots, these bamboos grow from his mind;
Without shoots, these bamboos are shaped by his brush.
By a deserted creek, beside a winding bank,
Two clusters, fifteen spears, dense and luxuriant;
Pretty like a girl with a softly powdered face.
I look up and suddenly forget it is a painting.
Inclined my ears to listen in quiet, I seem to hear their sounds
In the western corner, seven spears, vigorous and strong;
I clearly remember seeing them before a rock at T'ien-Chu monastery.
In the eastern corner, eight spears sparse and lean —
I recall having seen them in the rain at the Temple of the Goddess Hsiang.
Elegant airs, deep thoughts, are appreciated by few;
We look at each other, and I sigh in vain.
What a pity Master Hsiao is getting old,
His hands tremble, his eyes dim, his head the color of snow!
He says that this is his last painting;
From now on such bamboos will be the hardest to find.

TABLE OF CONTENTS

PROLOGUE

This is a story of two young people who met, fell in love, and married. That by itself is not unusual, but the two young people in this case were in China, and the time was a critical and violent period in that country's history. Others have analyzed the factors that led to the dynastic change that took place in 1949, or have described in detail the events that occurred. This account is not one of them.

Rather, this is a personal memoir, largely anecdotal, written for my daughters and grandchildren to tell them how their parents separately made their way to China, why they went, how they met, what they did there, and how the turbulent events taking place around them shaped all our lives in the years that followed. The telling of this story, in the context of the historical power transfer then taking place, often reveals how naive we were in many respects, and how confident and self-centered. While our lives were making an important transition, the country around us was also moving into a whole new stage of its long existence. The way we chose to cope with all this was not unlike the experience of other young Americans of our generation who ventured abroad for the first time midway through the 20th Century. The China we knew at that time was a totally different experience from what awaits the 21st Century visitor, and that is another dimension to the story.

This is also a story about how we came away from this with a great affection for China, its people, history, culture, scenery and, of course, the food. Reaching this stage did not come readily; the troubled times which this account covers produced many reasons for foreigners like us to become disaffected from, rather than attracted to, the land and its people. But the balance reached by the time of our departure was clearly most positive.

And finally, we tended to look on contemporary events as yet another dynastic change in China's history. The Nationalist government of the Kuomintang Party, under Gen. Chiang Kai Shek, used the southern city of Nanking as its capital. The Communist Party forces, under Chairman Mao Tse Tung, would use as their capital the beautiful north Chinese city known as "Peip'ing," a major historic and cultural center. In doing so, they would change the name back to "Beijing," which means "northern capital" and is the city's traditional name. The title of this book uses this name change to indicate the dynastic transition that was the background to the personal memoir.

Much of what is written here draws upon what we remember of people and events now more than 65 years in the past. In putting it together we talked with friends and acquaintances who were there at the same time, and whose recollections sometimes strengthened, sometimes differed from our own. For the period September 1947 to April 1948 we have letters written from Canton to Peip'ing; those from Peip'ing to Canton during the same period were lost in a shipment of personal effects that never reached the U.S. Finally, this account also draws upon details and dates from reports correspondents and other observers were sending from Peip'ing in 1948 and 1949.

The Chinese place names and terms used here are in the romanized Wade/Giles system, the form in widest use immediately after World War II. While this has now been replaced by the Pinyin system, this account keeps the older form because it seems more appropriate to events of that earlier time.

ACKNOWLEDGMENTS

An earlier version of this story, written many years ago, was dedicated to our three daughters, Nancy, Khati and Sue, and presented to them and our grandchildren at Christmas, 1993. In response to strong encouragement from "Mike" Vandeweghe, Mary Rowe and Nicole Lezin, that version was expanded to be published in this present form. The piece remains basically a family memoir, but now covers a longer span of time and ties our family's beginnings with events in our later lives.

Special thanks go to Nicole, however, for her invaluable help in getting the new draft into an appropriate format and shepherding it through the whole publishing process. Without her assistance this expansion of the story would never have appeared.

A few words about the cover are also appropriate. The painting was originally a work created by Brig. General Frank Dorn, then a young U.S. Army Aide to General "Vinegar Joe" Stillwell and stationed in the city once known as "Peking." The view is a uniquely detailed Map of Peking, illustrated with clever sketches of Chinese history and culture, which was sent to Gen. Dorn's friends as a Christmas greeting card in 1936. In the late 1980s, a surviving copy of the map was enlarged and reproduced into a museum-quality print. Gen. Dorn's family generously gave Mrs. Robert H. Moyer permission to run a limited printing of this piece, one of which I possess as Print #24 and have used as the cover to this book.

Elsewhere in the book there are pictures of Communist Army forces entering Peip'ing after its capture in early 1949. These appeared with a National Geographic article in Volume XCVI, No. 3, September 1949, and were taken by James Burke, then a freelance photographer living in the city.

CHAPTER ONE

"... on August 10,1946, President Truman had forwarded to the Generalissimo [Chiang Kai Shek] a personal message, in which the President had expressed his concern at the deteriorating situation in China and at the actions of selfish interests of extremist elements, equally in the Kuomintang and the Chinese Communist Party. The President described the growing conviction that an attempt was being made to settle major social issues by resort to force rather than by democratic procedures...

"The discouraging lack of progress toward a political and military settlement in 1946 was matched by a steady deterioration of the National Government's economic position. In contrast to the relatively bright situation prevailing on V-J Day, China, 16 months later, was gripped by a mounting inflation, its reserves of foreign exchange had been partially depleted, and no real beginning had been made on the task of internal rehabilitation and economic development."

United States Relations with China, [The "China White Paper"]
Department of State Publication 3573, 1949, pp. 179, 220.

San Francisco, September 1946

A former wartime transport vessel, the *Marine Lynx,* still in its battle-gray paint, had been waiting for days to depart for China and the Philippines with its passenger load of 408 American missionaries, and about an equal number of Asians. The date was September 1946. A dock strike had kept the vessel at its San Francisco berth beyond the scheduled departure, to the growing annoyance

1

and concern of the passengers, but clearance finally came and the long voyage to Shanghai got under way.

Among the China-bound passengers, but decidedly not in the missionary category, were four teachers traveling to Peip'ing [now called Beijing] to take up positions at the Peking American School (PAS). One of these was Lyn [*née* Grace Estalyn Kreps], twenty-five years old and with neither prior interest in, nor knowledge of, the Far East. The short answer to why she was on a ship headed for China is that she was very angry at the University of California at Berkeley and the San Francisco School system, and more or less in that order. The full answer is a bit more complicated.

During the war years, Lyn had been teaching in San Francisco's Aptos Junior High on a long-term substitute basis. She was a graduate of Stanford, and had completed the additional graduate year then required to obtain a California teaching certificate. Her substitute status was due to a wartime ban on new regular appointments to the San Francisco public school system, but once the war was over, and the ban dropped, she expected to receive a regular appointment.

She had really wanted to enroll in a doctoral program at the University of California in Berkeley, but had been discouraged by an interview there with one of the faculty. This professor told Lyn that, as he saw it, she had spent her life in an Ivory Tower; she not only came from an academic family, but had done little in life up to that point except attend schools or teach in them. In his opinion she ought to "live a little" before starting any graduate work, although given her academic and teaching record there was no way the university could turn down her application. He wound up this devastating assessment with the gratuitous observation that "she was probably a goddamned virgin to boot." A regular teaching appointment therefore became, if not her major career objective, at least the best alternative for the time being.

The San Francisco school system announced in the Spring of 1946 that qualified candidates could finally apply for regular teaching positions. Somewhat to Lyn's surprise, the published results of the written tests showed that she had scored the highest grade among the more than two thousand applicants who had participated. She also knew that her supervisors had written glowing letters on her behalf, and were genuinely supporting her candidacy. When the final rankings were announced, however, Lyn found she was 72nd on the list.

In a mixture of rage and dismay at this outcome, Lyn asked to meet with the Superintendent to get some explanation for what had happened. Since her low ranking had to be due to the interviews in some way, given the outcome of the other two parts of the screening procedure, she wanted to know what she had done to fail the interviews so miserably.

It was nothing she had said or done, the Superintendent hastened to reassure her, but the interviewers just felt she did not need a regular teaching appointment. They thought Lyn would probably get married and settle down soon enough, being a woman, whereas any male applicant would need a regular appointment to support an existing, or prospective, family. The Superintendent concluded by adding that the public school system would be delighted to continue Lyn indefinitely on a permanent substitute basis, but without retirement contributions, raises or any of the other benefits of a regular appointment.

Returning to the apartment she shared with two other young women, depressed, frustrated and angry, Lyn reported what she had just been told. At some point in this recounting Lee Shaw, one of the roommates, suggested: "Why don't you go to China and teach instead of just staying here?" Although this was a startling suggestion, it was not far-fetched. Lee came from a missionary background in China, had attended school there at the PAS, and her father was currently the head of the school's Board.

The PAS had recently reopened, and was looking for teachers to expand its faculty to a point where it could again offer a full twelve-year course of instruction. The Board had a serious recruiting problem, however. All it could offer a prospective candidate was a two-year contract, a round-trip passage to China, and $150 a month, hardly an attractive proposition even in those days. But Lyn was so thoroughly fed up with her situation in San Francisco that practical considerations somehow did not matter much. When Lee offered to write a letter to her father saying Lyn would consider going to China, Lyn's quick response was "why not?"

The process of getting ready to leave for China began that summer with visas, shots, selecting things to take along in the limited baggage allowed, and generally putting affairs in order for an expected absence of two years. By the time the day of departure finally arrived, Lyn's father was so angry and upset at her decision that he refused to see her off. A Stanford professor, and a man who had himself

3

travelled widely throughout the Far East in the early '30s, he was very concerned over his eldest child's plans. He had good reason to be concerned.

China, in the summer of 1946, was showing many signs of coming apart. The Nationalist Government, under Generalissimo Chiang Kai Shek, had moved its troops physically into key population, transportation and industrial centers throughout North China and Manchuria; Japanese troops had largely been disarmed and transported back to Japan; the U.S. military had assisted the Nationalists by airlifting troops and equipment to the new positions they were occupying. But as President Truman's note to the Generalissimo stated, the end of the war did not bring progress toward internal peace and economic revival. The Nationalists and the Communists had presented a common front against the invading Japanese, albeit an uneasy one of mutual suspicion and distrust. Once the Japanese were defeated, however, this common front collapsed; the two armed factions could not agree on a framework for working together within a national government during peacetime. All signs indicated their differences would ultimately be settled by a vicious civil war.

Lyn was not unaware that the situation in China posed risks of many kinds, but she was excited about teaching abroad and probably downplayed in her own mind some of the warning signs. In the end, parental disapproval did not change Lyn's decision, and when the *Marine Lynx* dropped its moorings she was on deck waving goodbye to the only family members who were present, a younger brother and his recent bride.

At Sea, October 1946

Passenger service across the Pacific was slow to be restored in the early post-war period. Two former troop ships, the *Marine Lynx* and the *Marine Adder,* were kept in service to fill the gap and meet the pent-up demand for trans-Pacific passage from missionaries, business people and displaced Asians who had spent the war years in the U.S. Although some attempt was made to convert the vessels to civilian use, it was a minimal effort and the accommodations were not much different from those the troops had experienced. Sleeping quarters were in the hold, bunks were four tiers deep, women and children were separated from men and boys; food was served military mess-style; little light or air penetrated the hold area. Some of the passengers, particularly the Chinese, began to be seasick even before the ship left the dock, and this situation became epidemic by the time the *Marine Lynx* hit the long Pacific swells that awaited just beyond the Golden Gate. Conditions in the crowded below-decks areas quickly drove Lyn topside, both to regain her own sense of equilibrium and to escape the smell and visible misery of her fellow passengers. She stayed above-decks for the rest of the long trip.

Before leaving San Francisco, Lyn met three other teachers traveling with her to Peip'ing. Two of these, Gen Shaw and Florence Mostert, were, like Lyn, in their twenties. Gen was going to teach the third and fourth grades, Florence the first and second. The third teacher was Ruth Kunkel, then a woman in her early fifties and a former nurse who had worked in Peip'ing pre-war. She naturally assumed the role of leader for the small group because she was both older and had already lived and worked in China. Ruth was to be a teacher of Latin. Florence had strong missionary ties, and quickly found she was more at home with the women and children in the hold. Ruth had no affinity for missionary company, but nevertheless kept to herself during the voyage, probably because of the age gap with her other colleagues. Gen was a different story. Young, attractive and outgoing, she also fled the hold and gladly joined Lyn on deck. There the two found a group of young men who were equally anxious to distance themselves from their elders and the crowded conditions below.

These young men were an interesting collection. All were associated with the Church of the Brethren, a Mennonite sect with strong roots in the Midwest, and all had been conscientious objectors during the war. Strictly speaking, they were not heading for China as missionaries, despite their church affiliation and sponsorship. Rather, having refused to participate in the destruction of war, they were dedicating a portion of their lives to the task of rebuilding a country that had been savaged by war. The approach was, in many respects, similar to the Peace Corps of later origin. The Brethren volunteers were going to a less developed country, in this case China, to teach rural people simple ways to improve their living conditions. It was an unselfish objective for its time, and the volunteers' goals were lofty, but this was no stuffy bunch of young Puritans.

As the days at sea melded one into another, the young people aboard stayed on deck and settled into a tight little group that kept pretty much to themselves.

The days and nights were clear and warm, so there was little need to go below except to eat and use the bath facilities. They read, played cards, sun-bathed, snoozed and in the evenings sang songs of the war and college years. Gen had a particularly clear and true voice, plus a sizable repertoire to add to songs the others already knew. And they discussed what they expected to find in China, how the hostilities might be resolved, and where their experiences might ultimately lead them. There was a diversion for two days when the ship's engines stopped, and the vessel drifted without power or rudder, but that was eventually repaired and the voyage continued.

On the other hand, life among the missionaries was much less harmonious. After all, 29 denominations were represented on board, with constant discord and bickering among them. They were unhappy about their accommodations, particularly those with wives and children who remained seasick and uncomfortable, and disagreements arose over when, in what order of precedence, and where they would hold their religious services. Almost all seemed to want, at the same time, the limited space on board available for holding meetings. The missionaries also resented the easy-going attitudes of the young group, whose singing and extrovert ways surely offended the more prudish and narrow minded. And so the voyage proceeded, with the two disparate groups in somewhat uneasy juxtaposition, until the *Marine Lynx* finally dropped anchor in the Whangpo River at Shanghai on October 15, 1946, and most of the passengers disembarked.

Shanghai, always known for its color, contrasts and excitement, was something of a jolt to newcomers just after the war. Certainly the confusion was great as ships unloaded and disgorged goods and people onto the famous Bund. To the inexperienced young teachers it was a heady, chaotic scene of milling, shoving people shouting in a totally unfamiliar language, with no obvious pattern or organization to any of it. Once they had cleared Customs with their hand luggage, they checked into the Palace Hotel, not far removed along the Bund from the Customs shed. They would return the next day to look for their hold baggage, which had been simply dumped in one enormous pile with the personal baggage from several other ships that had also recently arrived. Fortunately, Ruth had instructed her colleagues, before departure, to mark all their baggage with brightly colored stripes or unusual designs. This turned out to be a valuable tip. The four teachers could identify their trunks and boxes more readily than could other arrivals whose effects looked like everyone else's in the luggage mountain through which they all painfully searched. With their baggage finally recaptured, the group of teachers had another few days before they could leave for Peip'ing. There was a chance to see something of Shanghai, say goodbye to the Brethren volunteers before they took off for different parts of China, and then the teachers themselves left for Peip'ing.

CHAPTER TWO

"KALGAN REPORTED CAPTURED BY GOVERNMENT TROOPS"

New York Times, October 12, 1946, p. 1

"...U.S. General George C. Marshall and Ambassador Leighton Stuart have been impressed by the Communist threat that if Chiang Kai Shek took Kalgan the Reds would begin all-out civil war in a "total national split." For those who started from that premise, the fall of Kalgan held an unhappy political significance."

Time, October 21, 1946, p. 36

"This week Time's Nanking bureau cabled: "One fact is clear: a new and decisive phase of the civil war has opened. The greatest need for China is peace...but now it is possible and indeed likely that if China is to have peace, it can only be assured through a civil war fought to some kind of decision."

Time, November 11, 1946, p. 37.

Peip'ing, Late Fall 1946

The small group of teachers finally reached Peip'ing [which translates as Northern Peace] in late October. Formerly known as Peking [meaning Northern Capital], the city had been a capital for provinces, princedoms, kingdoms and empires since 1121 B.C. In 1264 A.D. it was made the capital of the Yuan [Mongol] Dynasty under Kublai Khan, and the Ming Emperor Yung Lo made

Peking his capital in 1421 A.D. The Ch'ing [Manchu] Dynasty ended its days here in 1911, and during its reign Peking was twice attacked by foreign troops, in 1860 and 1900. The second time was during the Boxer Rebellion, when troops were sent to rescue foreigners besieged within the city. The name was changed from Peking to Peip'ing when the Nationalist Government established its capital in Nanking [which means Southern Capital] in 1928.

By 1946, when Lyn arrived, the city had only a few of what could be called modern buildings. These stemmed mostly from the 1920s and '30s, and for the most part consisted of drab, gray offices, mission quarters, schools, hospitals and shopping areas. The rest of the city was made up of the magnificent remains of China's Imperial past — the palaces, massive city walls, imposing gates, temples and ceremonial places — and walled compounds within which lived much of the population.

Tucked away in all this, not far from the northeast outer city wall, was the PAS where the teachers were heading. The school was housed in a western-styled, brown brick building, with classrooms, an assembly hall with stage, labs and other particulars quite similar to U.S. schools built in small towns during the 1920s. PAS had opened on September 23rd with 192 students in attendance.

The number would rise, in the course of the school year, to 211 students, of whom more than half were Chinese, somewhere between one-quarter and one-third American, and the rest a mixture that contained fifteen nationalities — White Russian émigrés, some Japanese and Germans whose families had not yet been allowed to leave China, displaced persons from all over Europe, a few Turks, at least one Latvian, and students from various diplomatic families. The American students came mostly from missionary families or U.S. military families.

The PAS faculty, including the principal and the four most recent arrivals, totaled thirteen, of whom seven were Americans. Although the word "American" appeared in the school name, and the financing was underwritten by American organizations, it was a thoroughly international school in its makeup. Because Lyn and her companions had been delayed in their departure from San Francisco, the school had to start without its full faculty complement, and everyone was eagerly awaiting the arrival of the new teachers. As the 1947 PAS Yearbook describes it: "One afternoon toward the end of October all school was buzzing with excitement at news the four new teachers had finally arrived from Shanghai!

The next Monday a curious group of students, looking out from behind closed windows, watched old-time En Ling [the school's custodian since 1921] rush out to greet [them]."

Some of those who were peeping out the windows remembered it well, and described it to us years later as a time of great stir and curiosity. Everyone was enormously interested in what the teachers looked like and what they would wear, and were somewhat titillated to find them so attractive. Being not too much younger than the teachers in age, the female students in the high school were most impressed by the self-assured young women who approached their school that autumn day, and immediately identified with them.

The school that re-opened in the Fall of 1946 was first established in 1919. This was a remarkable place, both in what it was and what it aspired to be. Again citing the 1947 Yearbook, "Peking American School has been the sole institution in which students were trained to abolish racial and national prejudices, and on the other hand to promote mutual understanding among each other. Unlike some foreign schools in China, which try to install and infuse their faith and doctrine into the brains of students, and make them take up the bias and partiality of the schools, the Peking American School offers students free discussion and belief of individual conceptions and opinions in politics, religion and social views." This last comment was a poke at the doctrinaire mission schools of certain of the religious denominations and the German and Japanese schools that had operated during the war years, and which some PAS students had attended.

The then Principal of PAS was Alice F. Moore, described by her students as a woman of "...unparalleled enthusiasm, courage and capability." She had been with the school since it started twenty-seven years earlier. Kindly and courteous, firm when necessary, and wise beyond belief in the ways of students and mankind generally, Alice Moore and PAS were so intertwined in people's minds as to be virtually indivisible. During the Japanese occupation she was interned in the Wei Shen concentration camp, along with many other foreign nationals from countries at war with Japan. Not one to relax and drift with the adverse tides, Alice Moore quickly set up an improvised school using boxes as seats and charcoal for pencils and chalk. A few PAS classes actually graduated under those conditions. When the war ended in 1945, Alice returned to Peip'ing and began the task of restoring PAS to its pre-war status, an effort which led to the successful re-opening of the school in the following year.

The PAS, though small by most Stateside comparisons, offered a full program of instruction, kindergarten through high school, based on an American curriculum that prepared its students to meet U.S. college entrance requirements. Success in getting graduates admitted to U.S. colleges was what made PAS particularly attractive to those Chinese families financially able to meet the tuition costs, not to mention that a PAS education would make their children completely fluent in English. What the student body lacked in size it more than made up in esprit, and the school offered many extra-curricular activities: clubs, plays, sports (basketball, ice hockey, soccer, baseball and ping pong) and field trips. There were parties that Fall at Halloween and Thanksgiving, and Christmas was memorable because a U.S. Marine band from T'ientsin supplied the party music.

Lyn's assignment was to teach the seventh and eighth grades (which were, in fact, in one classroom), and American History to the high school students. She made an immediate and positive impact on her students. Having grown up in an academic family, with a father noted as an outstanding teacher and staunch liberal among the crusty conservatives of the Stanford Business School, she reflected that tradition. Lyn encouraged free discussion, particularly on controversial issues such as how to provide for the less fortunate, deal with bigotry and dogma, and ensure equality of opportunity.

Some of the students told us in later years this open approach to issues quickly got her identified as a radical, probably a Communist, by many students. Little wonder. Controversy was not a staple of nightly dinner table conversation in the homes of most military officers and missionaries, or traditional Chinese either for that matter. And some students had previously attended only schools where learning was by rote and where independent thinking was discouraged.

To students from such backgrounds Lyn opened vistas they had never imagined; for many, attending school suddenly became a uniquely stimulating experience. Several of them stayed in contact with Lyn over the years, and told us that of all their teachers she was the one who tried to teach them to think. Lyn set high expectations for them, and the students worked hard to meet them. But in addition, anyone guilty of inattention or sloppy work was soon made aware of it by something these students referred to as "the look."

A China Story: From Peip'ing to Beijing

Peip'ing was not all work and no play. At the time several thousand U.S. military personnel were still stationed in and about Peip'ing. Some of them, assigned to South Field, were the last of U.S. Marines originally sent to occupy the city at the war's end. Others, stationed at West Field, were U.S. Air Force personnel who formed part of the massive U.S. airlift. This moved Nationalist troops and equipment from the south to occupy strategic cities and rail facilities in North China and Manchuria as the Japanese forces withdrew. A smaller group was assigned to the Executive Headquarters of what came to be known as the "Marshall Mission." This was a U.S. effort to mediate the differences between the Nationalists and Communists and bring the two together in a single national government, and on terms both sides could accept. Officers assigned to this group were allowed to bring families with them, and many of these military dependents attended PAS.

Being young, single, attractive, American and female in a setting like that was a recipe for instant popularity beyond anything one could possibly imagine. And so it was at first, with officer's clubs at the bases, and a club in the Peking Hotel not far from Lyn and Gen's compound. There was dancing, American food, plenty of liquor and a large and constantly changing assortment of lonely, bored young men who had been away from home for a long time. Under the circumstances, it was not too difficult to have date offers from a different person each night stretching weeks ahead. The main problem was keeping the scheduling straight.

The frantic, always changing, social life continued up to about Christmas, when at some point Lyn paused long enough to ask herself where this was all leading. Most of the men she met were content to spend an evening at dancing and chit chat, often about the girls or wives who were waiting for them at home. A few were more aggressive, or had too much too drink, and became problems. But on the whole it was a transient crowd, people always coming or leaving, with no real friendship likely to emerge with any of the people she was meeting. Rather than let the pattern continue, Lyn decided to stop it, retire to being a teacher, and start to learn more about China and what was happening there. Though she did not know it, the fun and games were due to end shortly after the New Year anyway, when the military would be withdrawn, the bases closed, and the officer's clubs disbanded.

CHAPTER THREE

"On January 6, 1947, the President announced that he had directed General Marshall to return to Washington to report in person on the situation in China...The greatest obstacle to peace in China, the General stated, was the almost overwhelming suspicion with which the Kuomintang and the Chinese Communists regarded each other."

United States Relations with China, p. 217

"The United States Government has decided to terminate its connection with the Committee of Three which was established in Chungking for the purpose of terminating hostilities in China and of which General Marshall was Chairman. The United States Government has also decided to terminate its connection with Executive Headquarters which was established in Peiping by the Committee of Three for the purpose of supervising, in the field, the execution of the agreements for the cessation of hostilities and the demobilization and reorganization of the Armed Forces in China. The American personnel involved in the Executive Headquarters will be withdrawn as soon as possible."

Press Release issued by the Department of State, January 29, 1947

Peip'ing, Early 1947

Up to about the time of the New Year, it would be safe to say that Lyn had hardly left home. She was teaching an American curriculum at an American-style school, many of her colleagues were American, she lived in a comfortable

15

and well-appointed house with many amenities, her social life was almost totally bound up with American service men, and her neighbors were mostly American correspondents or business people. This was all undergoing gradual change, however, precipitated by the rapid withdrawal of the American military presence in Peip'ing.

Lyn was living at this time in a compound that Ruth had managed to find through her pre-war contacts. The word "compound" refers to residences that, in most cases, were originally the homes of wealthy, often titled, Chinese during the Imperial era. Compounds were composed of a series of connecting courtyards that stretched in a straight line back from the main entrance. In their largest, most expansive stages these compounds were the living quarters for extended families and their sizable retinues of servants, but over time, and with the wartime impoverishment of many of the original families, these compounds became subdivided into smaller units that were rented to outsiders, i.e., non-members of the family. It was such a smaller, sub-divided part of a once-larger compound that was rented by the new teachers.

One entered the compounds of Peip'ing through a front gate that opened onto a lane or alley known as a "hut'ung", a term used only in Peip'ing. Hut'ungs ran off either side of the main avenues of the city, sometimes in fairly straight lines in an east/west direction, but sometimes in mazelike twisting, turning patterns. All that one could see of a compound from the hut'ung was its wall, nondescript gray in color, and with paint and plaster in various states of repair. Some front gates were painted a bright vermilion, with polished brass door knockers and maybe polished brass fittings, indicating a wealthy family lived within. But some wealthy families, probably most, preferred to let their gates become weather-beaten and unattractive in order to mask the household's real economic status.

Once you stepped through a main gate you faced a "spirit wall," about eight to ten feet in height and extending in length beyond the width of the gate. The function of this wall was to prevent evil spirits from entering the household. Spirits were thought to move only in straight lines so if, by some chance, a spirit managed to penetrate the front gate it could not venture farther inside without running into the spirit wall. Ordinary mortals simply walked around one end of the spirit wall and proceeded into the compound immediately behind it.

16

A China Story: From Peip'ing to Beijing

The entry to Lyn's compound was through a gate from the hut'ung, behind which was the customary spirit wall. To the right, after you walked around the spirit wall, was a gate house, two-stories in height, and beyond that another wall. You stepped through this wall via a "moon gate," so-called because of its round shape, and into a paved courtyard, quite spacious and shaded with trees. Beyond this court was the main building of this part of the compound, the central feature of which was a large living/dining room with a fireplace. To one side was a bedroom with attached bath (where Lyn and Gen slept), and beyond that was Ruth's bedroom. The kitchen and servants' quarters were off the other end of the living room.

The furnishings belonged to a pre-war friend of Ruth's who had put them in safe-keeping when she fled China, and who was happy to let Ruth use them instead of keeping them indefinitely in storage somewhere. The living room lamps, couch and sofa were in an art deco style. A grand piano in one corner, done in gold lacquer, added a touch of elegance. In those post-war days there was great pressure for housing from people who had fled to the city from outlying areas, and landlords were fearful that unused parts of compounds might be forcibly occupied by unwanted, non-paying and probably destructive, squatters. The Chinese gentleman who owned this compound was therefore more than willing to lease a part of his much more extensive domain to three foreign teachers, and at a modest rent that even they could meet out of their ridiculously small salaries. All in all, it was an extremely favorable, comfortable, and rather grand arrangement.

In a variety of ways, Lyn was beginning to be aware she was living in a different culture and in a city that offered exciting new experiences. She began to pick up some of the language. It was, admittedly, a variety of "kitchen Chinese" that enabled communication with servants, shopkeepers and pedicab drivers, but it worked. As she travelled back and forth between home and school, she used the most available form of transport available, a pedicab. This was a three-wheeled, pedal-powered cycle with a driver in front and usually a single passenger behind. One bargained over the price of any trip in advance each time, partly because there was always a contest to see if the foreigner would be foolish enough to pay a very high fare, and partly because the real cost of everything was rapidly rising in the mounting inflation. Foreigners always paid more than Chinese passengers because they were less skilled in bargaining, but even so the fares were ridiculously cheap.

Although Lyn had already stopped the social life linked to the U.S. military presence, there was no easy alternative to it because the number of foreigners in Peip'ing who were young and non-military was still quite small. Something of a social vacuum therefore arose. This was not a total vacuum, since there were other amenable faculty members (a few) and neighbors, but life was not as busy as it had been.

Meeting Chinese was difficult. Not many situations existed where it was possible to meet young Chinese informally, and even then there was often a language problem that kept conversation at the level of the weather, how much one liked China (or the U.S.), and where one was born. Chinese who did speak fluent English, and who were outgoing in personality, often proved to be people it would be better to avoid. Many of these were anxious for foreign contacts who could get them a trip to the States, provide access to U.S. military stores, exchange money, or buy whatever they were selling.

One exception to this came on a day in the late Fall of 1946. A young man who had been among the Church of the Brethren volunteers aboard the *Marine Lynx* and who was then living and working near Peip'ing appeared at Lyn's compound with a young Chinese woman in tow. She was introduced as Miss Lin, a secretary in the office of Gen. Yeh Chien Ying, Chief of Staff of the Chinese Communist Army. Gen. Yeh and his staff were part of the Communist delegation to the Marshall Mission peace mediation talks then underway. Miss Lin was anxious to meet young American women, something she found difficult to do until she was sent to Peip'ing for the peace talks. In Peip'ing it became possible to meet foreigners, and she wanted to learn what she could about the U.S. She already spoke quite good English.

The two women hit it off immediately and spent a good deal of time together. Miss Lin was particularly amused that their names were so alike, Lyn and Lin. On several occasions she invited Lyn to have dinner at the Communist headquarters and meet some of the key figures there who were engaged in the negotiations. Unfortunately, Lyn never accepted these invitations, and lost a rare opportunity to meet some prominent newsmakers. What Lyn did get from Miss Lin, however, was a first hand account of the civil war from the point of view of someone totally engaged on the Communist side.

Lyn heard Miss Lin's stories of peasant life in China, its hardships, the poverty associated with greed and misrule, and the sufferings due to years of war against Japan. The Communists were portrayed as pursuing a campaign to free the country from Nationalist rule, something people in the countryside readily supported.

This interpretation was, in fact, gaining credence within China. Evidence of the shortcomings of Nationalist rule and the ineffectiveness of its military efforts was visible everywhere. The true state of affairs in areas under Communist control was less easy to judge because communication across the lines was very limited. In any case, rumors circulating in cities like Peip'ing were increasingly more favorable to the Communists than to the Nationalists. One heard, for example, that Communist troops dealt fairly with people in the rural areas, did not impress labor for their needs, did not loot and pillage as they moved through the countryside, and were actively providing medical care and education in villages that had never had them before. Lyn enjoyed knowing Miss Lin, and hearing how she sized up what was happening in China, but the contact ended abruptly. The peace talks broke down, Miss Lin left Peip'ing, and Lyn never heard anything more from or about her.

Peip'ing, Late Spring 1947

The school moved into the final phase of its second term, and the class routines and round of student activities continued pretty much as usual. But there was also change in the air. While the last group of students had arrived in early January, the Army dependents were scheduled to leave in mid-March, in the wake of the failure of the Marshall Mission's mediation efforts. And Alice Moore had celebrated a birthday in April by announcing that she was ready to leave China to visit relatives for a year, since she had not been back to the U.S. since her imprisonment at the Wei Shen camp.

The departure of the Army dependents was marked by a Farewell Tea Dance arranged by the Senior Class in early March, but some were still around at the time of the Easter party. The gap the dependents were expected to leave was intimated in the Yearbook's description of that event: "On the third of April the [PAS} had its Easter party. It was organized by the Juniors under the direction of June [Ch'en], their president. Despite the pessimistic prophecies of the organizers, the party was a real success. There were plenty of couples to dance, enough refreshments...the lights went out only five times, the Marine band played many old favorites and played them loudly...Everybody had a swell time...The party lasted until 11:30 p.m. when many of the kids were brought home by one of the remaining Army buses. It was lots of fun Juniors, thanks ever so much!"

Some of the military dependents, bemused by their own sense of importance, confidently predicted that PAS would have to close without their continued attendance. But Alice Moore used the occasion as a statistics lesson to demonstrate to students in math class that military dependents had always been a relatively small proportion of the student body, and the national composition of PAS, in percentage terms, would barely change after they had gone.

Alice Moore's birthday was celebrated with an impromptu serenade and the presentation of a gift when she emerged from class on April 15th. Her impending departure naturally raised the question of who would replace her, and Lyn was Alice's choice of person to stand in for her as Principal. In the short time she had been at PAS, Lyn came to be recognized as a first-rate teacher, a popular teacher, and someone who had earned the respect of her colleagues. The Board of the school unanimously agreed with Alice's choice, and made a formal offer to Lyn in writing, dated April 30, 1947. Lyn was not convinced. She was still young, totally inexperienced in administration, and could see one major problem from the outset.

Lyn told the Board she was flattered by the offer, but could not accept it. She was certain Ruth would never work willingly under her administration, although she would be content to work under Ruth's. The obvious solution was therefore to choose Ruth as interim Principal. Ruth's prior China experience and her age were additional factors to be considered, although she had proven to be neither a strong nor well-liked teacher up to that point. In the reluctant view of Alice Moore and the members of the school Board, there was no other viable candidate on the faculty, and it would be prohibitive to recruit someone from the U.S. as acting principal, particularly given the conditions developing in China. In the end, Ruth was appointed Principal for the coming school year.

A China Story: From Peip'ing to Beijing

The lovely Peip'ing Spring was turning to Summer, classes came to an end and vacation started. China was obviously in ferment, but superficially things still seemed normal. Lyn was getting to know more about China, enjoying what she was doing, and looking forward to a new school term in the Fall.

Lyn on board the *SS Marine Lynx*

Lyn with PAS student

PAS faculty in 1946; Lyn in foreground

Lyn and Gen in compound courtyard

Lyn and Gen in compound living room

Lyn visiting Chinese village

CHAPTER FOUR

> *"In 1947 the strategic initiative passed from the Government to the Communists and the latter carried the conflict from Manchuria and North China into areas which had supposedly been cleared by the Government. Activity which marked the turning point in the strife included the mounting by the Communists of a series of minor offensives in Manchuria and the successful blunting of a major Government drive into Shantung ...The Consul General at Mukden on May 30,1947, forwarded the following appraisal of the situation to the Department of State:*
>
> *"In past two months morale in Nationalist forces has deteriorated at rapidly accelerating pace...It is reflected in jumpy nerves of military garrison, efforts to evade conscription, and reliable information from all sectors of Nationalist territory...indicating that Nationalists in a panicky state are feverishly building trench systems everywhere...There is good evidence that apathy, resentment, and defeatism are spreading fast in Nationalist ranks causing surrenders and desertions."*
>
> United States Relations with China, pp. 315-316

New York, April 1947

At this point in the story let me introduce myself. My name is Jim Hendry, twenty-five years old at the time, recently demobilized from the army after four years of active duty, much of it spent in military intelligence Japanese language programs and the last several months of it in Japan. After three months of job hunting, and a chance contact through a friend from pre-war college

23

days, I had been offered, and accepted, a job with the Standard-Vacuum Oil Company (Stanvac) to spend three years in China as an executive trainee, usually referred to as a "classman." At last I was employed, the job promised to be exciting and interesting, and in a part of the world I was anxious to see again. Life seemed good, and my mood buoyant.

Stanvac in those days was a company jointly owned by the Standard Oil Company (New Jersey) and the Socony-Vacuum Oil Company (New York). This was a marketing/production joint venture by two companies who could not engage in it legally within the confines of the U.S. because of the anti-trust laws, but could do so overseas. Since it was formed in 1933, Stanvac had developed producing and refining capacity in the Dutch East Indies, and engaged in marketing operations throughout the Far East, South Asia and parts of Africa. In 1946, the company began the process of rehabilitating its damaged production and refining facilities, and was making efforts to regain and expand its marketing share in areas where sales of petroleum products had been disrupted by war. A popular novel of the 1930s, "Oil for the Lamps of China," was based on the pre-war adventures of Americans engaged in selling kerosene in China, and it was generally understood that the fictional company for whom they worked was modeled on Stanvac.

The top managers at Stanvac had always been Americans, and still were at the start of the post-war era. At the other end of the marketing chain were the up-country agents who actually sold the petroleum products, and were Chinese. In between these two extremes was a layer of Stanvac's Chinese employees who provided the link between managers and the agents, roughly analogous to the role played by non- commissioned officers in the military. These were the people who made the wheels hum. They worked smoothly and effectively with the local Chinese business communities to develop a marketing network, meanwhile satisfying the foreign managers that all was being done properly. Like noncoms in another sense, they were expected to stay in their place. These able, talented and extremely knowledgeable men never expected to move into a top management post. That was to be reserved for the classmen being sent out post-war, of which I was one. Classmen were to receive on-the- job experience in all aspects of the company's business so that, in time, we would move into the upper layers of management above the Chinese staff. The system had worked well in the past, and in those immediate post-war years the system was expected to work well again in the future.

The job as a Stanvac classman was very attractive. Most of those going into these assignments pre-war had done so directly out of college when, in the words of a Stanvac recruiting circular, "...applications are considered only from American citizens, between the ages of 21 and 25, who have secured the written consent of their parents." Those of us applying in 1947, in contrast, were in the age range of 25 to 30, had completed three or more years of military service, and many had spent part of that time in combat overseas. Parental consent was certainly never asked for nor given in these latter cases, even assuming anyone had bothered to think about it, which nobody did. The pay was very good for those days, particularly since there were no professional qualifications for the job. In addition to a salary in dollars and free living quarters, the company provided a monthly cost-of-living payment in local currency that was geared to the rate of inflation.

There was, however, one small condition, clearly set forth in the circular in these terms: "Applicants must be college graduates and single, although there are no objections to marriage after the employee returns home on first regular furlough. These qualifications are basic from which the Company does not deviate... No written contract of engagement or service is made, but it is mutually understood that men assigned to Foreign Service will, at the discretion of the Company, remain abroad for at least the service period of three years."

This did not seem a very onerous condition to me when first I learned of it. With no romantic attachment at the time, I saw little likelihood one might materialize in a place like China. This was not true for all the classmen, however; some were already engaged, and for them acceptance of a Stanvac offer meant enforced separation and deferral of marriage plans for three years. The company had some valid reasons for this policy pre-war, particularly when considering the immaturity and lack of experience of many classmen of that era, but the policy no longer made much sense in the post-war recruiting environment.

Five of us, from among a larger group in the company's New York-based training/orientation course, were slated to go to China — Sam Strassburger, Bill Wells, Jack Reardon, Joe White and I. Sam had fought in North Africa and Italy and was engaged to be married before joining Stanvac; Bill had studied Chinese in the army and had seen service in Burma and China; Jack and Joe had been in the Marines together and had fought in the Pacific.

When the training course in New York ended, Bill and I were asked if we would each take a new Chevrolet sedan with us into China as part of our personal effects. This involved the company "selling" us each a new car for one dollar so that it could be registered in our names. The car would be re-sold to the company in Shanghai for the same amount after taking delivery of it there. The reason for this subterfuge was that the Chinese government refused to release foreign exchange for the importation of cars by companies doing business in China, but individuals going to China could bring in a car for their personal use. Cars for official business use were much needed in China, so Bill and I agreed to this arrangement. This meant we, and our cars, would travel to China on a freighter, rather than go with the others on one of the former troop transport vessels.

In early May, our training course completed, we took possession of our new cars and set out for California. Since Sam preferred to drive with us rather than traveling across country by train, the three of us left together and took turns with the driving. The trip cross-country was not very eventful, although we travelled through parts of the West that were new to me. By traveling steadily, without stopping to sightsee, we reached San Francisco by mid-May. Bill and I loaded the cars aboard the *SS Midnight,* a freighter bound for Shanghai and Hong Kong. Sam, Jack and Joe, unencumbered by cars, left separately on the old *Marine Lynx,* still in the service of carting civilian passengers across the Pacific. We did not meet again until we were all in Peip'ing.

A trip by freighter still sounds like an interesting way to get somewhere, particularly on a vessel with a name like the *SS Midnight.* The name alone conjured up for me Hollywood-fed fantasies about high adventure in the mysterious East. When I first caught sight of our ship at the Embarcadero dock I half expected to see Sidney Greenstreet emerge from the cabins, cast a wary and suspicious eye on the loading activities, and return below leaving a trail of cigar smoke. He did not appear, of course, and my remembrance of the voyage is that it was much less exciting in fact than it was in prospect.

Five passengers besides ourselves were aboard: an attractive widow and her small son and a British police officer with his dowdy wife and young son; all were headed for Hong Kong. The captain, rather than turning out to be Humphrey Bogart, was a Dane with a mania for playing bridge. He spent the first few days trying to engage Bill and me in a nonstop game that could have continued for the whole trip. After a couple of rubbers, which gave us a chance to sense how good a player he really was, we both found more compelling things to do. Had we been foolish enough to go along with his suggestion, we might have found our first year's salary mortgaged before we got off the ship.

The passage turned out to be an easy one, and the food was not too bad, but it was a dull trip. The cramped space available to passengers consisted of our cabins, a narrow stretch of deck along the cabin area, and a small salon/dining area. This left little room to do much of anything, especially exercise. Fortunately, Bill had anticipated this, and at his suggestion we had come prepared with a large selection of books. It was pleasant at first to talk to the lovely widow, who had lived in Hong Kong before the war and was anxious to return, but her obstreperous son managed to interrupt any conversation we started. The stuffy British police family we rather fended off when our paths crossed, but they did not pay much attention to us, either. In the end, we gradually gave up trying to be social and retired to our books as the best company available. The gooney birds soared constantly over the stern of the ship waiting for the sporadic disposal of garbage over the side, the days were filled with sunshine and warm breezes, the engines chunked steadily along, and after nineteen days we arrived in Shanghai.

Shanghai, June 1947

I can still recall the excitement felt when approaching China, and have never had a travel experience to match it. We approached the coast well after nightfall, and one could smell the land long before actually spotting it. When we awoke in the morning our ship was riding at its berth off the Shanghai Bund, surrounded by boats of all sizes and descriptions propelled by people selling things, ferrying things, or simply standing by to see what happened next. The June morning was hot, but despite that the scene we looked down on below us was so new, so noisy, so confused and so fascinating that it was with effort we finally pulled ourselves away from the ship's rail and completed our packing for disembarkation. This was what I had come abroad to see, and the first glimpse was meeting all my expectations.

As we made our way to the Customs Shed to clear ourselves and our baggage through, including the cars, the disorganization that Lyn had found the year before was no longer so evident. At least it did not seem unduly chaotic to us, but we also had the advantage of being met by Stanvac employees whose job it was to clear new arrivals through the Customs process, and they were very good at what they did. Not too long later, therefore, we had all our luggage in hand and were also taken to the Palace Hotel.

After the high excitement of our initial introduction to the waterfront and port activities, the old Palace Hotel was a letdown of sorts. The war years had not been kind to it. You could still see traces of once elegant woodwork and fine fittings, and the public rooms were large and high-ceilinged, but everywhere there was the look and smell of decay and indifference. Paint was peeling, furniture was worn, carpets were shabby. We realized we should not expect too much when there had been so many years of hard usage and minimal maintenance, but it was two years since the war had ended and there was still little sign anyone had plans to rehabilitate and refurbish the place.

This somber mood was reinforced as we began to move about the city. The streets were crowded with people going about their business, the traffic an exotic mixture of autos, busses, trucks, bicycles, pedicabs and rickshaws. The latter made a particularly cruel spectacle. Ragged, sweating, emaciated men in the traces pulled high-wheeled vehicles in which sat large, prosperous-looking people, oblivious to the appalling contrast they made. There were also lots of beggars, pitiable figures all, but the women with babies and small children were the most startling and painful to see. Whatever I may have read before about famine and starvation in China did not prepare me for the shock of the poverty and human misery now visible all around us. Police trucks were said to travel through the city streets daily at sunrise to pick up the bodies of beggars who had died during the night hours, and from the condition of many we saw this was quite believable.

The first item of business was to check in with the Stanvac main office soon after we had settled into the hotel. The paperwork associated with turning over the cars was completed, we were introduced to a number of the key people in the office, Americans and Chinese, and we were given the details of our first assignment. This would consist of three months during which we would receive Chinese language training in Peip'ing, and for this we would depart in two days' time to assemble in Peip'ing with a number of other Stanvac classmen. These were either due to arrive shortly, like Sam, Jack and Joe, or were men who had been in China for some time and already working in branch offices scattered throughout the country.

This was good news because a prolonged stay in Shanghai was not an attractive prospect, and we were anxious to get on with things. Bill already had a command of Chinese, from his earlier army language training and experience in the country, but I was uneasy in a place where I could not understand what people were saying. The school experience therefore seemed a great way to start my Stanvac career.

During our visit to the Stanvac office several people suggested we drop by the American Club if we were at loose ends for the evening. Since this pretty well described our status, Bill and I decided to set out after dinner to see what the club had to offer. Bill knew his way around Shanghai a bit, and could negotiate with pedicab drivers to take us to the club and get us back. Left on my own, I doubt I would have ventured out of the hotel at all. Looking back on that evening, the specifics are difficult to recall, but our overall impressions still remain vivid.

At first, the club seemed an island of newness and order that contrasted favorably with the dinginess of the Palace Hotel and the unease of the city. As the evening progressed this mood quickly changed. The people we met seemed to be straining to have a good time. Their conversation was loud, and its content banal and centered on their perks, their possessions, and local foreign community gossip. The club servants were ordered around with an imperiousness that we newcomers found jarring. Efforts to get people to talk about what was happening in China got nowhere, although after three weeks of isolation aboard ship we were eager to hear the views of people who were living and working in China.

Out of all this came the distinct sense we were with a very insular bunch of people, privileged beyond imagination compared to most Chinese living in the city outside their club walls, superficial in their values, and disinterested and indifferent to what was happening all around them. Not too much of this was needed to decide the time had come to leave, and we rode back to the hotel in a depressed silence. The contrast between what we had just seen and the mean street

29

sights we passed through was so great there seemed little we could say. In time familiarity would breed an acceptance of much that upset us that night, but at the moment we were powerfully affected.

The next evening, our last in Shanghai, we were invited to have dinner at the residence of Stanvac's General Manager, and for this occasion a company car called for us at the hotel and returned us after the meal. The house and grounds were spacious and lovely, the furnishings mostly Chinese and very tasteful. A courteous and well-groomed servant directed us to the lawn at the rear, which was as lush and trimmed as a putting green, and there we met the General Manager and two of his higher-ranking subordinates.

After introductions all around, and preliminary comments on the agreeable weather and the attractiveness of the setting, the GM noted that the sun had indeed sunk below the yardarm and it would be all right to have a drink before proceeding to dinner. When the drinks arrived, the GM pursued the yardarm theme a bit more by noting the importance of keeping one's drinking within bounds. Young men, he observed, were inclined to let themselves go in a foreign environment, and if they did not impose some self-discipline they could soon find themselves in serious trouble from over-indulgence. That was why, the GM continued, he never allowed himself a drink until the day's business was over. This little sermon was obviously intended as an object lesson, and turned out to be the major one of the evening.

At dinner the conversation stayed mostly at a level of pleasantries, inquiring into our backgrounds and prior experience, and talking a little about the old days in pre-war China and the difficult times some people had at "up-country" stations. I do not recall any serious discussion about the current situation in China, or even its implications for the future of Stanvac's operations. Perhaps company policy at the time was to express no doubt publicly that the Nationalist regime would prevail in the struggle then taking shape. This would, at least, be consistent with the cautious attitude the company took toward any issue, and could explain why the GM and his aides made no serious effort to sound out Bill and me on our views and impressions on arriving in China.

But what I really remember most about the evening was the dismay I felt at seeing for the first time a full dinner setting of silverware, probably eight or nine pieces in all. The dining room itself was imposing, the service quietly impeccable, and I was trying to make a good first impression on the most important men in my incipient career. In my confusion, and despite my general understanding that one worked from the outermost pieces toward the plate, I reserved the fish knife for the meat course because it looked sharper than any other knife in my setting. If anyone else noticed my gaffe they did not say anything, but I felt my cheeks redden when it became obvious I was the only one at the table wielding the wrong implement on his roast beef.

The next day we departed for Peip'ing on a China National Airlines (CNAC) flight. The trip was short and comfortable. Not flying at a high altitude by current standards, it was possible to see the countryside below pretty well. The country itself looked hilly, dry and unproductive, not the lush green rice paddy lands I had expected. We arrived early in the evening, and after some waiting and indecision at the airport, a rickety, dusty airline bus appeared and took us to town. There we were deposited in front of the (closed) airline office on Morrison Street, and without further ado the bus just disappeared.

The sun had set and dusk had fallen on the city. There were few people about and the traffic in the streets was light. Compared to Shanghai this was serenity and peace, and our spirits rose in response. Peip'ing, at first sight, justified its name "northern peace." Bill's knowledge of Chinese was again invaluable, since no one from the airline was around to provide assistance, and he quickly commandeered two pedicabs to take us to our destination, the Hotel Wagon Lits in the old Legation Quarter.

The evening was beautiful, warm and soft with the touch of early summer. Pedicabs, with small lanterns burning on the handlebars, looked like fireflies in the growing dark as they moved through the streets. The only sound to disturb the quiet was the tinkle of pedicab bells warning of their approach to an intersection, or signaling they wanted a right-of-way. The trees in the Legation Quarter were all in leaf, the streets dimly lit, and in the gloom of dusk everything looked very European, clean, orderly and attractive. We had arrived in Peip'ing, and it was a great relief to be there.

CHAPTER FIVE

> *"By mid-summer the Communists had started a southward movement... toward the Yangtze. This process, at first an infiltration rather than a general movement, forced the Government to abandon some of its gains in Shantung... In commencing this movement south while the Government had large forces concentrated in Manchuria and Shantung, the Communists were operating on what appears to have been an effective appraisal of Nationalist intentions and capabilities, a realization that the Government was committed to positional warfare, was overextended, that for reasons of prestige it would not withdraw or consolidate, and that mobility and the initiative lay with their own forces. By late 1947 the Communists had concentrated such a considerable force in Central China that only a major Government offensive could have dislodged it."*

<u>United States Relations with China</u>, p. 317.

Peip'ing, Summer 1947

My meeting with Lyn started so casually, accidentally. The day after Bill and I checked into the Wagon Lits we were in contact with the local Stanvac office. The then district manager for Stanvac in Peip'ing was Neil MacFadyen, a man who had grown up in China as the son of missionary parents and spoke fluent Chinese. He and his wife Ruth bade us a warm welcome, and Neil quickly briefed us on what to expect during our stay in Peip'ing. Two bachelor establishments were being set up to house and feed us and the other dozen or so Stanvac classmen coming for language training; we could leave the hotel and move into the one to which we were assigned in a day or two. Classes at the language school would start shortly, as soon as everyone had arrived, and would continue until September when we would receive our assignments to Stanvac branch offices throughout China.

For a few days, therefore, not much was on the schedule, and after dinner that evening Bill and I decided to walk around the Legation Quarter and orient ourselves to our new surroundings. The Legation Quarter, established originally to house the diplomatic corps accredited to the Chinese Imperial Court, was not a large area. Only three long blocks in length and two blocks wide, it was enclosed within crenellated high brick walls and surrounded on three sides by a bare, sandy tract known as "the glacis." Houses and shops that once stood outside the walls had been leveled after the Boxer uprising of 1900 to create a field of fire for defenders of the embassies in the event the Legation Quarter were ever attacked again; the area remained empty in 1947. The fourth walled side, to the south, fronted on the railway line instead of a glacis. Four gates gave entry into the quarter, one at each end and two through the walls on the north side. Since Nanking had become the capital of China in the mid 1920s, these former embassies housed foreign representatives of less than ambassadorial rank; the U.S. compound, for example, contained the residences and offices of a Consulate General and the Foreign Service Language School.

As we strolled that evening down the Quarter's main thoroughfare, Legation Street, we made a left turn into Marco Polo Street and found, halfway down the block on our right, the once prestigious Peking Club. Because the gate to the club was open and unguarded, we decided to go in. The clubhouse ahead of us was a large and imposing building, but needing paint and care. Since no one was around, we took a look inside. All the expected facilities were there — a bar, library, reading/meeting rooms and a dining room — but all were empty of either staff or members, and all looked rather dusty and shabby. Outside the clubhouse were tennis courts, also vacant, and back toward the main gate a swimming pool. With so little going on in the clubhouse area, we ambled toward the pool. To our surprise, we heard splashing noises in the pool and the unmistakable sound of female voices.

Approaching the pool's splash area we were hailed by two young women, with distinctly American accents, who were swimming in the pool. They said, as I remember, things like "Hi," and "How are you?" We replied with repartee equally sparkling, asking things like "How's the water?" The water was, we were assured, just fine. Since the last thing we expected to find that evening was two young American women in Peip'ing, let alone in the Peking Club swimming pool, the next obvious question was who were they? They told us they were teachers in the PAS, but I do not recall they told us their names. One, of course, was Lyn, and the other Gen. We, in turn, identified ourselves as Stanvac "boys," but without offering our names, either.

Somewhere in the discussion one of them asked why we did not try the pool. This struck us as a great suggestion on the face of it, but there were drawbacks. For one, we were not members of the club, but more importantly we did not have bathing suits with us. Bill and I looked at each other, hoping one might have a bright idea about how to respond, when at that juncture two young men emerged from the men's locker room, dove into the pool, and joined the women.

The newcomers were introduced as also members of the PAS faculty. Though Lyn later disclaimed they were dates of theirs, Bill and I assumed they were and began to make departing noises. Wishing them a pleasant swim, and expressing hopes of meeting them soon again, we left the club and returned to the hotel. This had certainly been a casual meeting, almost anonymous since we did not even learn each other's names, but it was the first meeting. Neither Lyn nor I were much impressed at the time, but from my perspective things began to look as though a modicum of social life might be found in Peip'ing after all.

The next week suddenly became busy. Other Stanvac classmen arrived and we all moved into the bachelor quarters provided for us. Bill and I were assigned to a compound on Wu Liang Ta Jen hut'ung (the Street of 52 Big Men), which ran east off Hatamen Street, one of the city's main north/south thoroughfares. Sam, Jack and Joe, with whom we had attended Stanvac's New York training program, had also arrived and were assigned to a second bachelor's mess, located closer to the language school. To fill in the time until school started, an overnight visit to T'ientsin was arranged for the Stanvac group. The purpose was to introduce us to the terminal facilities there, and demonstrate key elements in the storage and handling of petroleum products.

Getting there and back involved a two-hour train trip each way, which in itself was not a problem, but that particular rail line was being cut by Communist forces with increasing frequency, usually by blowing up a bridge or section of track. Nationalist troops, manning little mud forts, were guarding the bridge crossings. This was obviously ineffective in thwarting or deterring attacks, however, which usually came at night. Little injury or loss of life resulted from these disruptions because they occurred before the trains arrived, but the attacks could disrupt service from several hours to a day or more, depending on the nature of the resulting damage. The local press referred to these events as the work of "bandits," but no one believed this and assumed, correctly, that it was due to a significant Communist presence in the area.

Once back from our field trip, we started our language training at The College of Chinese Studies (Hua Wen Hsueh Hsiao). This had long been a major center for instructing newcomers, mostly missionaries, in the northern dialect, known as Mandarin, which constitutes the official language of China. Our initial instructor was Henry Fenn, another China-born former missionary whose father was the noted author of a well-respected Chinese/English dictionary. Major emphasis in class was on the spoken language, with little or no effort spent learning to read Chinese characters.

Chinese is a tonal language, and the Mandarin version uses four tones. The meaning of a word is determined by which of the four tones is used. The grammar, on the other hand, is simple and the word order not unlike English. Our daily drilling was therefore mostly on getting the tones right and building a vocabulary. Afternoons were ample time to study for the next day's class, so no evening homework was really necessary. Because Bill already had a good grounding in Chinese, he was allowed to pursue an independent study program that did emphasize reading and calligraphy. Classmen from the Shell Oil Company (British) and the Caltex Oil Company (a joint American venture of the Standard Oil Company of California and the Texaco Company) also began language instruction at the College, though in separate classes.

As the summer wore on there were new additions to the foreign community, mostly American, and these were people from diverse backgrounds doing interesting things. Besides the oil company classmen already noted, a number of Fulbright students began arriving about the same time, as well as a few other scholars on grants to study some aspect of Chinese life or culture. The State Department had a Chinese language school housed in the Consulate General compound, and the U.S. Army stationed a few officers in Peip'ing to pursue language studies independently of the State Department program. Students in both of these groups were allowed to marry and bring spouses with them, since the course of study was usually for two years or more. The number of correspondents also seemed to grow that summer. Some of these were regulars whose bylines and publications were familiar; others were stringers looking for the chance to come up with a big story that would make a reputation for them.

Another sizable group was engaged in intelligence activities, a residue of the wartime OSS organization that had recently been disbanded. There was still need to continue an intelligence-gathering function, however, given the deteriorating state of relations between the Nationalists and the Communists. A group known as the External Survey Detachment (ESD) was doing just that. Some of these people were in uniform, some in civilian clothes, and all had access to vehicles, commissary goods and other advantages most foreigners in Peip'ing lacked.

There were visiting instructors at Yenching University and Tsing Hua University, both located outside the city walls, and the PAS added three new people to its staff. One of these was Dorie Eldred who, like Lyn, had been recruited from the U.S. She was a recent graduate from Occidental College in California, and was slated to teach in the elementary school program. The other two were the Scott sisters, Ellie and Barbie, who were in China accompanying their father, a visiting professor at Yenching for the upcoming Fall term. Since neither had finished college at the time, they served as assistants in the library, or as general helpers in the principal's office, not as teachers. Finally, there were people who were opening, or re-opening, business offices in Peip'ing, some who were staying with parents or relatives, and others who were just coming for a prolonged stay to observe at first hand what was happening in China.

The advent of the Fourth of July supplied an occasion for a social event that could bring together a large slice of this young American community then assembling in Peip'ing. The movers and shakers for this were two remarkable women, Mary Ferguson and Helen Beaumont, who had lived in China most of their lives. They were sisters, children of an illustrious father who, among other things, had once been the president of Nanking University. Mary was Secretary to the Board of the Peking Union Medical College, China's preeminent medical school; Helen, the widow of a U.S. Marine general, was residing in Peip'ing with Mary in the large and exquisitely furnished Ferguson family compound. Between them, these ladies possessed a vast store of zest, intelligence and charm. With the help of Marian Clubb, wife of the American Consul General, the two sisters decided to throw a large Fourth of July party at the swimming pool of the American compound in the Legation Quarter. This was to be an opportunity to mingle and meet other people, and everyone who came took full advantage of it. The main drawback was that the group was mostly male.

As I looked around to see who was there I spotted a familiar face, again in the swimming pool. This was Lyn, but on this occasion I also had a bathing suit. Since she seemed by herself, I got into the pool and made my way toward her. Catching her eye, I opened the conversation with: "Say, aren't you one of the Peking American School teachers?"

This was, admittedly, not a very brilliant conversational gambit. It was the best I could think of, however, and I hoped it might sound like the query of a sophisticated man of the world, one who was not quite sure of the answer. "Yes," was the reply and, with a strong tinge of sarcasm in her voice that reflected what she thought of my left-handed approach, Lyn added "and aren't you one of the Standard Oil boys?"

This deflated my confidence considerably, but I persevered and somehow, from that unpromising conversational start, we did progress to other matters and even finally exchanged names. Neither of us has ever been a particularly strong swimmer, and the reason for being in the water at all that day was the heat of the July afternoon, so it was not long before we were out of the water and meeting and talking with other people.

The details of that afternoon are now very dim, but I am sure I introduced Lyn to several of my Stanvac colleagues. She, in turn, introduced us to colleagues of hers and to people she had come to know over the period she had been in Peip'ing. Again, I am not certain we made much of an impression on each other, but the ice had been broken and I recall now only that it was a fine party and we all enjoyed ourselves immensely.

Once the Fourth of July party had brought people together, there began to be parties and social gatherings that built on the introductions made there. One of the popular places was a former officer's club, the roof garden atop the Peking Hotel, just down the street from T'ien An Men Square. Small groups of Stanvac people would go there with Lyn, Gen and others for dinner and dancing on weekends. People gathered at the Peking Club for tennis, swimming and sometimes official cocktail parties. The bachelor messes of the oil companies also gave frequent parties for all who were available, and the ESD compound was a popular party place because their commissary access enabled them to entertain on a more lavish scale than others. These were not "dating" situations, because most people did not attend in couples. Rather, they were like the college "mixers" given at the start of a term, before people know each other very well. People had a chance to dress up, do something light and entertaining, and it offered a welcome change from the company and food of the bachelor compounds.

One evening, on a weekend toward the latter part of July, there was a large party at the ESD compound, much like others. Lyn was there, and during the evening we had danced some and talked some while having a bite, a drink, or a cigarette together. We had not come to the party together, but as the evening grew late one of us, and I cannot remember who, suggested it was time to leave. The party had reached a noisy stage where it was not much fun, and seemed unlikely to get any better. We both felt the same about it, obviously, and when I offered to escort Lyn back to her compound she accepted.

Leaving was not difficult, and doubtful we would be missed at all, so we soon found ourselves riding down Hatamen Street in a pair of pedicabs. The drivers kept abreast of one another so that we could talk, which was the usual practice when traffic was as light as it was that evening. At some point in the journey something happened that we both remember vividly, though neither of us can remember what triggered it. Lyn was leaning forward slightly in her pedicab, chattering about something, when suddenly she turned and said that if she were ever to marry she would like to marry a person like me.

Perhaps we had been talking about the lack of serious romantic interest in either of our lives; Lyn had been engaged before and had broken it off long before coming to China. Maybe we were talking about the Stanvac requirement that classmen remain single their first tour abroad, or gossiping about the young men then in Peip'ing, and how superficial so many seemed at first meeting. Whatever we had been talking about, the main thing I remember, of course, was the sudden jolt of surprise, pleasure and excitement that Lyn, this very attractive and popular person I had met so recently, could think of me in such terms.

From that evening on the situation changed decisively. We began to see each other regularly, not always as part of a group now, and certainly more frequently. The more we saw of each other, the more I came to realize that, in addition to her attractiveness, Lyn added qualities of intelligence, wide-ranging knowledge and a fresh, frank, outgoing personal manner that others simply lacked. For these reasons alone I could feel pleased and flattered that Lyn would be willing to spend time with me, but that was not all — she was totally unlike any woman I had ever known and, simply, I was completely smitten.

I should note at this point that I had grown up on the eastern end of Long Island, New York, in a rural community that was certainly no center of intellectual ferment or curiosity, and where most people in prewar days had only limited awareness of the larger world around them. Their political views were conservative, their outlook narrow, and their interests limited to their own or their neighbor's business. Lyn's effect on me was thus much the same as it was on her students at PAS — stimulating, challenging and new. This is not to deny or downplay the boy/girl attraction that was part of it, and a very strong part of it. But, I had never dated anyone before who stimulated my mind as well as my emotions, and this was a completely different and exhilarating experience.

A popular Rogers and Hart tune called "Manhattan," from the Broadway show "Garrick Gaieties" (1925), concludes the refrain with the lines:

> "The great big city's a wondrous toy
> Just made for a girl and boy,
> We'll turn Manhattan
> Into an isle of joy."

And that is pretty much what we did with Peip'ing during the swiftly passing weeks of that lovely summer. Peip'ing was a wondrous toy. Roughly rectangular in shape, Peip'ing contained the remnants of four distinct cities within its outer walls. The northern two-thirds was known as the Tartar City. At its core was the Forbidden City, a palace compound for the Imperial families. Adjacent to it was an area called the Imperial City, reserved for Manchu officials at the Ch'ing Court, the last Imperial dynasty. The rest of the Tartar City was originally for Manchu troops, their families and retainers. Finally, south of the Tartar City, and separated from it by interior city walls, was the Chinese City, where the ethnic Chinese were expected to reside.

This was our plaything, and we set out to make the most of it with all the enthusiasm and stamina of the young. The Legation Quarter, most mission establishments and other foreign offices and residences were in the Tartar City, and indeed the compounds where Lyn and I were living were in this part of the city. Just down the street from Lyn's compound was the Tung An Shih Ch'ang, a large indoor market with odd and wonderful things for sale. A Mongolian restaurant, where you grilled your own meal on large braziers, was set atop the roof. When done to one's taste, the meat was dipped in a delicious basting sauce made from exotic condiments supplied by the management. The Chinese opera was nearby, but one performance convinced us this was not habit-forming, and we did not return for another performance. Some of the most spectacular sights, such as the lakes of the Imperial City, Coal Hill, the Dagoba and Ch'ien Men (the Tartar City's Front Gate), were also in the Tartar City, as were more mundane attractions such as the Peking Club's swimming pool, the French bakery, the White Russian delicatessen, the movie theater and the up-scale stores that specialized in rugs, prints and expensive curios.

But the Chinese City was the lively part, filled with crowded lanes, shops, restaurants and all sorts of intriguing activities. There were popular restaurants that served only Peking Duck, and streets where the shops specialized in furniture, or pearls, or jade, or silver, or almost whatever one might want. Non-specializing restaurants were everywhere, all of them good and serving the flour-based, pungent cuisine of North China. These we visited with friends because Chinese food is best when eaten with several people seated around a table, and with a large variety of dishes to share.

For something out of the ordinary, even in Peip'ing, there was the evening the two of us decided to visit the Jade Market. From what we had heard, this was a wholesale market, little known to foreigners, where dealers came from all over northern China to buy and sell jade in all stages of processing. The market was reportedly located somewhere in the Chinese City, and did not open until three o'clock in the morning. Something as mysterious and exotic as this sounded too good to miss, so one evening we stayed up late enough to make the effort to find it.

Neither of us had any particular concern about wandering through the back streets of a Chinese city in the middle of the night, though I realized lack of sleep would make it hard to get through the next day's classes at the language school. We found pedicab drivers who said they knew how to find the Jade Market, and after a few false turns and dead ends we did wind up at the site. Alas, the stalls were empty — we had picked the wrong night of the week for a visit. As we headed back toward the Tartar City, the first light of day appearing over the compound roofs, our disappointment at missing the market was somewhat offset by the knowledge we had actually tried something others had only talked about.

Some distance outside the city walls was the famous Summer Palace, a rambling conglomeration of a lake, covered walkways, buildings, and artifacts built to divert Imperial minds from the heat of summer. This was a favorite spot to visit, and not far from there was the Jade Fountain Pagoda, water source for the lakes in the city, and a lovely setting for picnics. We also picnicked at the Temple of Heaven, took excursions into the Western Hills, and made a luxurious visit to the Great Wall by train, sipping tea and eating cookies in the dining car on the return trip. The summer really was the best of times, in the best of places, and we had only begun to exhaust the possibilities.

Peip'ing, August 1947

The days passed quickly, of course, but a couple of notable events provided a departure from the calm routine of language school and the pleasures of sampling the attractions of Peip'ing. The first was a decision by Lyn and Gen that together they visit the Tat'ung caves, situated near the city of Kalgan in Chahar Province, about 150 miles northwest of Peip'ing.

Kalgan had been recaptured by the Nationalists the previous October, and was being somewhat tenuously held by them on the perimeter of areas they claimed to control. The caves were famous for the large number of Buddhist statues intricately carved from the rock inside. The caves, at least those lowest in height, could be seen and entered from the valley floor. The site was remote, the security situation highly uncertain, but the scenic and artistic rewards from visiting the caves were reportedly considerable.

A China Story: From Peip'ing to Beijing

I was unhappy about the trip. For one thing, it meant not seeing Lyn for several days, and that was an increasingly important consideration to me as the summer passed. The other factor was the inherent danger for two young women to be alone in a relatively isolated area where fighting could be renewed at any time. I expressed my misgivings, and tried to persuade Lyn to put off the trip, but things between us had not yet reached a stage where I felt I could invoke any proprietary interest in her decision. Actually, the whole venture sounded pretty interesting, and I would have gone along but for the language classes.

The trip began as scheduled, with a train ride to Tat'ung. Once there, Lyn and Gen stayed with a Swedish missionary family who lived and worked in the area. The caves were as spectacular as advertised, some so high up in the cliffs that the two could not climb up to them. The Swedish missionaries were another matter, grimly self-righteous and minimally hospitable, and after one night's stay with them Lyn and Gen decided to leave and visit Kalgan to see what could be seen there.

On the train platform in Tat'ung they ran into the Fenn family, comprising at that point Henry, the head of the College of Chinese Studies, his wife, and twin sons who were students at PAS. The meeting was totally unexpected by both parties, but since they were all going back to Peip'ing by way of Kalgan it was logical that they combine forces and go together. Henry Fenn, for his part, was dismayed that Lyn and Gen, with limited Chinese language skills, were traveling about in that part of the country on their own.

The combined group arrived in Kalgan late in the day, after dark had fallen, and learned there were no rooms available to spend the night. With Henry Fenn's skillful persuasion, however, and his superb language skills, an inn keeper grudgingly allowed them to use the stage of a small theater in his inn as a place to spread their sleeping bags. The problem was they were not alone there; other travelers seeking shelter for the night were also allowed to stay in other parts of the theater. By this time it was cold and raining, and there was not much to do, so the foreigners huddled together on the stage and even sang some songs, to the amusement and bewilderment of the Chinese who were sharing the theater with them. Using the toilet posed a problem. There was only one, and it was in steady and unrestricted use. To deal with this, Henry Fenn and his sons stood guard while the women availed themselves of the facilities, thus defending the cause of modesty and averting any unpleasant incidents that might have arisen.

Kalgan did not offer much in the way of sightseeing the next day, either. The place had the air of a frontier outpost, surrounded by hostiles, and the nervous population was neither prepared for, nor interested in, providing assistance to casual foreign tourists passing through. It did not take long for Lyn, Gen and the Fenns to decide that the next train back to Peip'ing was their best option. In retrospect, seeing the caves was worth the effort, but the kindest thing one could say about the night's stay in Kalgan was that it was unusual. Given the cold, and the uneasy tension that surrounded their being there, it was an experience one could easily forego. Had the Fenns not so fortuitously appeared, of course, things might have turned out much worse.

The second event eventually affected Lyn's housing arrangements, but came about as the culmination of several other developments. The problem had its origins in Ruth's materialistic orientation and her interest in adding to her income by exploiting lucrative opportunities as they arose. Her focus was increasingly on things Chinese, for the situation in Peip'ing that summer was such that bargains could be had if one recognized value when it appeared.

Ruth did know good items when she saw them — embroidery, textiles, prints, carvings, jewelry. On one occasion she urged Lyn to buy a Chinese gown, which Lyn did not particularly like, because the borders of the sleeves were decorated in a fantastically intricate type of embroidery known as "Peking Stitch." This method had been banned since the fall of the Empire because it ruined the eyesight of the women who produced it, and good examples of the forbidden art were thus becoming increasingly rare. The gown proved to be a wise purchase, though all but the sleeves were quickly discarded; the lovely stitched figures and floral design were salvaged, and have remained a prized possession.

In pursuit of her new entrepreneurial interests, Ruth drew to the compound a steady stream of Chinese merchant/traders, itinerant peddlers who went from door to door with all kinds of curio merchandise. From bundles that seemed bottomless, they drew out wares that were then spread on the floor in front of a prospective customer. If that produced no sign of interest, the peddlers went back to their bundles and came up with even more things for inspection.

One of Ruth's most frequent merchant visitors was a man named Robert Wu. Robert had moved beyond the stage of bringing a bundle with him, however, and instead would discuss with a customer particular items that might be of interest.

He would later appear with a selection of items that met what he believed were the customer's requirements. Robert's English was good, he had a prosperous appearance and was always well dressed, but there was something a little too obsequious and disingenuous about Robert Wu.

Gen was then dating a young ESD pilot named Bob, who was a frequent visitor to the compound. We never knew exactly what his duties entailed, but he did fly to Shanghai from time to time in a small plane, probably on some sort of courier run. By virtue of his uniform and the plane he was flying, Bob did not go through Customs when he left the air field to go into the city, either in Peip'ing or Shanghai, and this was generally known in our small community.

One day, as we learned later, Bob stopped by at the compound to see Gen and ran across Robert Wu, who was visiting Ruth as he often did. In the course of general conversation about nothing in particular, Robert Wu asked Bob if he would be willing to do him a favor by taking a small but rather valuable package to a friend in Shanghai. The mails at the time were so unreliable that he, Robert Wu, was reluctant to depend on them. Since Bob would probably be traveling to Shanghai sometime soon anyway, would he mind delivering the package to the friend at one of the major hotels? Robert Wu would pay Bob US$500 when the package was safely delivered, to compensate for any inconvenience that might be involved.

Bob accepted the offer. Sometime later, perhaps a week, Bob returned and we found him one afternoon storming around the compound in tremendous outrage. As he told it, his plane encountered some motor problems en route to Shanghai, and he had to land in Nanking because he could not complete the trip as planned. Bob therefore had to take the train from Nanking to Shanghai, and en route he began to wonder what might be in the package he was carrying for Robert Wu. In particular, he began to wonder what Shanghai Customs officials might find, since he would not be given the automatic clearance he normally received when flying into Shanghai. Bob decided to see what the package contained, and after carefully unwrapping the paper he found the package full of a white powder. I doubt Bob knew enough about narcotics to identify one when he saw it. He assumed the powder was a drug such as heroin, though, and it frightened him enough that he did not hesitate to throw the package and its contents from the train.

We found it hard to be too sympathetic with Bob, who was loudly castigating Robert Wu for treachery and double-dealing. Why, we wondered, would someone be willing to pay US$500 for a favor if there were no element of danger and/or illegality involved? Bob could not have been naive enough to think from the start that all was proper. His anger must have stemmed solely from the knowledge that Robert Wu had placed him in an unforeseen dangerous situation when Bob's Customs immunity unexpectedly disappeared. Robert Wu maintained the powder had simply been some Chinese traditional medicine, unavailable in Shanghai; since Bob did not actually know what the package contained, he was on shaky grounds in making his drug trafficking accusations. Nevertheless, it was a disquieting incident, reflecting badly on Bob, Robert Wu, and ultimately on Ruth as Robert Wu's friend and sponsor.

This particular event took place after Lyn and Gen had returned from their trip to Tat'ung and Kalgan, but even before then Lyn had been telling me of her uneasiness about the way the compound living arrangements were working out. Established at the start as a cooperative venture, each of the three teachers paid one-third of the rent each month, and they also divided the costs of servants, heat and utilities, and running the kitchen. Ruth, as house manager, provided scant accounting of how the household money was actually spent, however. Lyn harbored some suspicion that the amounts used for living expenses were on the high side, but as they remained in the affordable range she did not question the accounts very seriously. In addition, Lyn and Gen had each given Ruth US$500 for safekeeping, their reserves to be kept for emergencies, because Ruth had a strongbox in her bedroom. Since there had been no need to draw upon them until then, one assumed the reserve funds remained intact.

Over and above money matters, personal relationships within the household had soured considerably. Ruth was aware that Lyn had been everyone's first choice to be acting principal in Alice Moore's absence. While Ruth would actually serve in that role during the approaching school year, her jealousy of Lyn, and of Lyn's standing among their school colleagues, remained a constant irritant that exacerbated frictions that accompany any sharing of a household and its responsibilities.

Perhaps even more importantly, Lyn grew increasingly resentful of Ruth's efforts to use her and direct her social life. This went back to the earlier days when Ruth saw Lyn and Gen as means of access to the Marines and Air Force service men they were dating, and thereby to the goods available in the commissaries on their bases. As I became a steadier visitor to the compound, it became increasingly obvious Ruth neither liked me nor welcomed my presence. Ruth was quick to tell Lyn she was wasting her time seeing me so often. There were more promising prospects around, both financially and from a status point of view, and Ruth felt they would all benefit if Lyn cultivated some of these instead. In Ruth's eyes, I was not only too young but I was also the "marrying kind," a variety of man to be avoided at all costs. These opinions, when passed along by Lyn, simply reinforced my own negative feelings about Ruth, and fueled my growing concern over Lyn's housing situation.

While this was building to some sort of crisis point, a newly arrived teacher, Dorie Eldred, had arranged to share living quarters with the Scott sisters. Their large and comfortable compound, at No. 1 Fang Chia Yuan Hut'ung [Garden of Fragrant Excellence], was actually quite close to PAS. Lyn had written to Dorie several times, offering advice on what to bring and what to expect when she arrived in China, and was thus a familiar contact for Dorie once she arrived in Peip'ing. As the summer days passed, Dorie often turned to Lyn to discuss some of her adjustment problems, and Lyn in turn shared some of the misgivings about her own living arrangements. In the course of these conversations, Dorie mentioned that the house she and the Scott sisters shared had a vacant third bedroom, and Lyn would be a welcome addition if she wanted to make a move.

When I learned that housing as favorable as the Fang Chla Yuan compound was available, I began to press Lyn to make the move as soon as possible. Although the Bob/Robert Wu incident had shaken Lyn, she was reluctant to make an open break with Ruth. I was anxious that the situation be resolved before I left Peip'ing. The internal atmospherics in Lyn's compound bothered me a great deal; they were certainly unpleasant, possibly dangerous, and could only get worse. Lyn finally agreed with me, and approached Gen to see if she, too, would be interested in moving. For some reason, still not clear to us, Gen declined.

At that point only the notification to Ruth remained, and this was accomplished in a chilly, tense meeting toward the end of August. Lyn then asked Ruth for the $500 that was being kept for her in the strongbox, and was told that it had been "lost" in some venture involving the purchase and resale of PX goods acquired in T'ientsin. Since Lyn had never been asked whether she approved the use of her money for such a purpose, the failure to hand over Lyn's reserve funds amounted to a simple theft.

Though Lyn decided to do nothing about it, and in truth there seemed little that could be done, this final example of Ruth's cupidity convinced Lyn to move away. The transfer of personal effects took place before the end of August. Moving was no major problem because Lyn brought so little with her to start with, and had not acquired much else in the interim. I felt greatly relieved when it was all done. The new arrangement looked to be a happy one for Lyn, and also removed a potential source of worry for me when I left Peip'ing for my next Stanvac assignment.

Peip'ing, September 1947

The memorable summer was bound to end. Fall term started at PAS, and the easygoing days of vacation for Lyn evaporated in a new round of classes, course preparations, and grading papers. The language classes ended too, leaving our group at best slightly able to converse in Mandarin, and we received our new assignments. Stanvac offered the classmen an opportunity to express preferences, and I had chosen T'ientsin, naturally, as the place closest to Peip'ing, and Lyn. What I received was not T'ientsin, however, but Canton, the farthest place I could be sent from Peip'ing and still be in China.

This was not accidental. Neil MacFadyen had watched my interest in Lyn grow increasingly serious over the summer. Although a friend to both of us, Neil was aware that such a romantic involvement could be adverse, both from the company's perspective and to my own career prospects. His responsibility, as local Stanvac manager, was to see that classmen finished their initial language study assignment satisfactorily and were ready to move to their new assignments. When he strongly urged the Canton assignment for me he was probably reasoning the distance would serve to cool things a bit, and maybe even each of us would meet someone different.

The news of my assignment was disappointing, but not a surprise. Lyn and I could see the company's logic behind it, and to some extent we agreed with it. As the time to leave approached, we took stock of where things stood between us.

Our interest in each other had intensified as the summer passed, but we were very aware that what we felt could be illusory. Summer romances, particularly those in strange and exotic settings, were known to be fragile things. Were we really in love? What did we really know about one another, about each other's families? How would we strike each other if we had met back in the U.S.? One thing certainly different between us was our political orientation. I had become far less conservative over my college and war years, but was still no ardent liberal. Lyn, on the other hand, was an outspoken and articulate advocate of liberal views. I thoroughly enjoyed talking, discussing, arguing things with Lyn, and felt I was learning a great deal, but would she tire of trying to educate me? If I were to stay with Stanvac, could Lyn really stand being a company wife?

Thus we approached the parting time with sadness and strong affection for one another, but without any further commitment. We would write, we agreed, and I warned Lyn that the letters might be irregular because I had always been an unreliable correspondent. Lyn promised to return any letters I did manage to send, and hoped I would find Canton an interesting place. Maybe a visit could be arranged sometime in the near future, but the situation in China was uncertain at best, and we left it that we would just have to wait and see. There must have been farewell parties in the bachelor compounds, and Lyn and I must have attended them, but I do not remember details. I only recall that I was leaving Peip'ing sadly, and a much different person emotionally than when I arrived only three months earlier.

Lyn and Jim at Jade Fountain

Lyn and Jim at Jade Fountain
with Bill Wells and Zoe Clubb

Lyn and Jim with friends
at Summer Palace

CHAPTER SIX

"Most disheartening features of present Chinese situation in economic as in other spheres are overt reliance on a deus ex machina of American aid to extricate China from its pressing problems and corresponding lack of self-reliance and self-help in tackling them...continued passivity in the face of mounting hyperinflation clearly reflects a dominant trend of dependence on outside assistance."

Letter from the Ambassador in China to Secretary Marshall, dated September 20, 1947, reprinted in United States Relations with China, p. 831

COMMUNISTS CUT PEIP'ING-HANKOW RR NEAR PAOTING; CLASH WITH GOVT. OUTPOSTS 10 MILES SOUTHWEST OF PEIPING

New York Times, October 13, 1947, p. 10

U.S. ARMY FORBIDS PERSONNEL TO RIDE SHANGHAI-NANKING RAILWAY BECAUSE OF COMMUNIST ATTACKS

New York Times, December 14, 1947, p. 3

Peip'ing to Canton, October 1947

On the morning of the day I was scheduled to leave Peip'ing I arose early, picked up Lyn at her new compound, and walked with her to school. We made our gloomy goodbyes there in the schoolyard, and I trudged back through the hut'ungs to my own compound to finish packing and wind up last minute details.

After a hurried and definitely somber lunch I left for the train station with Nate Zimmerman, a Stanvac classman with whom I would be traveling, and who was being stationed in Hong Kong. By evening we were in T'ientsin. We were to leave the next day but, an hour before our ship was scheduled to leave, the dockside police discovered a flaw in my visa.

For twenty minutes or so the police discussed with each other whether I could re-enter China on my particular visa. Since I could now understand much of what they were saying, I stewed on the sidelines trying to edge into the conversation and possibly fix things up. Matters such as this were all handled at the Police Station, I was told, and unfortunately at the hours of 1 to 3 p.m. all the policemen were out to lunch. The ship was supposed to leave at 2 p.m., but the dockside police just could not see how I might be allowed aboard. At this point, the shipping line officials finally intervened, and after some more conversation one of the dockside police took me to the Police Station himself. There the whole matter was straightened out with a few stamps of an ink pad, the transfer of a picture of me, and $1200 CN [Chinese National currency, probably worth US$5, or less]. We were back at the ship by 1:45 p.m. and I was finally permitted to embark, though for a few moments I thought I might get a few extra days back in Peip'ing after all.

The coastal freighter Nate and I boarded was the S.S. Hanyang, about 8,000 tons, and bound for Shanghai, Foochow and Hong Kong. The ship flew a British flag and was captained by a genial drunk who, from the glassy stare in his eyes, must have been drinking since breakfast. Like all large vessels in the China coastal and river shipping trade, the Hanyang was fitted with steel bars to seal off the main passenger cabins from the rest of the ship; the decks inside these bars were patrolled by armed guards, mostly Sikhs from India. The purpose of this arrangement was to prevent pirates, who sometimes shipped aboard as deck passengers, from rushing the wheel house and main cabins and taking the ship.

Besides ourselves, the passenger list included a Protestant missionary, three wives on their way to join husbands somewhere, and two Catholic priests. One of the priests was going home to France for the first time in sixteen years. He had an amazing goatee, and a limited command of English. The other priest was an American named Murphy, fat and jolly, and strongly addicted to cigars and alcohol. He told us that his Bishop's first remark, after he came out of the concentration camp where he had lost fifty pounds, was: "Good, now stay that way." Father Murphy had obviously ignored this advice over the intervening two years. To the disappointment of Nate and me, we could not find two others among this company who were willing to play bridge.

The trip down the Hai River from T'ientsin to T'aku Bar was unexpectedly pretty. The fields were all green and brown, the villages neat and tidy, almost prosperous-looking despite the fact they consisted of mud huts and dirt lanes. Trees seemed more numerous than they were around Peip'ing, and everywhere one could see large stacks of grain and seed corn set out to dry on the roof tops; children waved and shouted as the ship passed by.

The leg from T'ientsin to Shanghai took four days, with a smooth passage most of the way and one moonlight night calm and very beautiful. After arriving in Shanghai we made our way to the Stanvac head office where our trunks had been stored, retrieved them, and brought them back to the ship to take with us to our new assignments. We spent overnight on the ship, and awoke the next morning to the strains of "God Save the King" as flags were raised on a British cruiser anchored next to us. We heard that a typhoon was hitting the coast near Swatow, and might require us to hole up somewhere to ride it out, but that did not delay our departure.

Two days later the S.S. Hanyang dropped anchor in the river that leads to Foochow and again stopped overnight, this time to load tea. The ship was surrounded by sampans and junks in a matter of minutes, until they were lined up six and seven deep all around. The noise and confusion were wonderful — dogs barking, babies crying, men and women screaming at each other while jockeying their boats into good position for boarding us. The wind and current were strong, and the boat people used their boat hooks with such disregard for eyes and faces and legs that we were almost afraid to watch. The sampans were surprisingly neat and clean, freshly painted and handsome-looking, and their owners brought food for our deck passengers, who gobbled up what was offered and generally had a fine time with the local residents. The Foochow anchorage itself was quite appealing. Mountains were in the distance, some coming down to the water's edge, with green fields in the valleys, and a slight haze that made the boats, the river and the background all blend together in an attractive collage. In the afternoon Nate and I went ashore in a sampan and walked through the hills until we

came to a pagoda. The grounds were littered with the ruins of walls and buildings, but you could see that the place had once been a lovely spot. More walking
brought us to the remains of the town where the Chinese Naval Academy was
once located. Many brick buildings, wrought iron gates and paved streets lined
with trees still remained, but the Japanese had destroyed all the main buildings.

We were again struck that people looked happy and well-off; a good deal of
boat building was going on and shops were filled with food. The women also
seemed much prettier than the northern Chinese. Their features were clean cut,
and they had beautiful white teeth. Even the coolie women wore flowers in their
hair, which they combed in a style that had bangs in front separated slightly like
the fringe on a rug. There really was not much time to explore Foochow, however,
and we were quickly under way again.

Now that I was actually on my way to my first posting I was beginning to
wonder, as the trip progressed, what it would be like to work for Stanvac. The
company's main appeal until then had been as a means of getting to China, rather
than the work itself, and I had not really given the job's content much serious
thought. As I now pondered it, I almost convinced myself the future might be
lots of fun, my new colleagues a great bunch of people, and the job interesting.
But then, I wondered, why would it be more fun selling kerosene than, say, vacuum cleaners? The answer was not immediately obvious, however, and I pushed
the whole train of thought back into my subconscious and concentrated on enjoying the trip.

The ship reached Hong Kong on October 7th, eleven days after leaving
T'ientsin, and fortunately no sign of the typhoon on the way. My first impressions were decidedly mixed; some aspects seemed to live up to Hong Kong's fabled
reputation, but in other respects the city was a disappointment. The setting, however, was striking. The city rises from the harbor as do the hills that overlook the
Bay at San Francisco. The commercial center, just off the waterfront, was very
British in style and tone, and the stores were stocked with anything one might
want. But the Hong Kong I was seeing for the first time was not the bargain
hunter's paradise it later became; prices were not cheap, and the radio-phonograph
I bought cost more than I expected to pay for it. The Peninsula Hotel on the
Kowloon side of the harbor, today still one of the world's grand hotels, struck me
as barn-like, gloomy and slightly shabby. On balance, Hong Kong was as close to

home as one could find in the Orient, if that's what you were looking for in the Orient. There was no opportunity to find out more about it, however, because at 1:30 the next morning the river boat for Canton left Hong Kong. Six hours later we arrived at Canton, the city I had travelled half way around the world to reach and start a new career.

Canton, Fall of 1947

The trip from Hong Kong was made in company with the manager of Stanvac's Hong Kong territory, a Mr. Pearson. Stanvac organized its China marketing operations by territories, each quite sizable and each centered on a major city. The territorial offices were in turn divided into smaller district offices, and Canton was such a district office within the Hong Kong territory. Mr. Pearson was thus my second level manager. Hong Kong served as a territory headquarters because the volume of petroleum product sales there for shipping, automobiles and aviation was large compared to other cities in China proper, Shanghai excepted. But the Canton district itself was also huge, extending from Hainan Island in the southeast, along the Indo-China border to the south, and on to Kunming in the west; this included the provinces of Kwangtung, Kwangsi and Yunnan.

The Canton district manager, Bill Watson, met us at the dock. The Customs confusion seemed definitely worse than usual to me, but with the two taipans [big bosses] present and watching, the Stanvac employees helped spirit us through in record time. That bit of business completed, we went first to the Watson apartment where Mr. Pearson would be staying, then off to tour the city and see how the company's affairs were being handled. We covered a fair amount of territory in the course of that day, looking at this and that company operation, but I understood little of what I was seeing. Finally, about 5:30 p.m., the touring came to an end and I was free to go to my apartment. My first glimpse of this was a brief one earlier in the day, but now I had some time to unpack and get my bearings before returning to the Watson's for dinner. All in all, a most tiring first day.

My home and the district office in Canton would be on an island called Shameen, originally a sandy mud flat on Canton's waterfront on the bank of the

Pearl River. After the Opium War of 1840-42, foreigners were not allowed to settle anywhere in the city, but were confined to this separate area set aside just for them. A handsome residential section arose there, sometimes referred to as the "International Settlement," and the Shameen I now found was what remained from that period of isolation and confinement for foreigners.

The island was lovely and quite small, taking no more than an hour to walk completely around it. Two foot bridges connected Shameen to the mainland, but no autos, pedicabs or rickshaws were allowed onto the island. The offices of most major foreign companies, banks, and consulates were located there, and the houses and apartments were occupied mostly by foreigners. A broad walkway, shaded by tall banyan trees, ran down the center of the island and served as its major thoroughfare. No stores, restaurants, movies or other commercial ventures were on the island, other than the venerable Canton Club that served as a gathering center for some members of the foreign community. Shameen was fortunate to have lots of trees, lawns and gardens, and the big Colonial-style buildings still retained a trace of former grandeur in their pillars, huge iron gates, and shuttered verandahs. All was quiet and clean, an oasis of western suburbia in the heart of a large Asian city.

The apartment provided me by Stanvac was to be shared with another classman, Ron Carey, who was away from Canton at the time I arrived. He was on a trip visiting up-country Stanvac agents since September, and was not due back until the following week. The trip would have been longer, but some of his itinerary was cancelled because bandits were active in parts of the region to be covered. The apartment, once I had an opportunity to look it over, was on the ground floor of a waterfront building facing west toward the river. Crowds of sampans were moored along the bund in front, and in the evenings the lamps aboard were lighted and tantalizing smells of food cooking drifted ashore. A lawn and trees separated the apartment building from the bund, and the apartment itself contained a verandah, living room, two bedrooms, two baths, a kitchen and, most amazingly, a refrigerator that made ice cubes. Nothing grand as a place to live, but every room had a fireplace and the apartment itself had plenty of space. Basic furniture such as beds, dining table, chairs and a sofa came with the apartment, but anything else that would make a place livable, such as lamps, rugs, desks, occasional chairs and tables, and wall decorations, would have to be furnished by Ron and me.

A China Story: From Peip'ing to Beijing

The day after my arrival was October 10th, the "double-ten" holiday celebrating the birth of the Chinese Republic. Since the office was closed, I had a bit more time to settle into my new quarters. All day long the firecrackers popped, the streets were decked with banners, and people everywhere seemed to be having a good time. The papers were full of news about a new Communist offensive in the north, and the possibility that the Nationalists would fall back on Peip'ing. Canton seemed very far away from all that, however, and it was far too early for me to form any opinion about the local political scene.

I liked Canton from the start. Not only was Shameen a pretty and tranquil place to live, but the main city was filled with shops that lined narrow, cramped streets, each with all kinds of fascinating things for sale. Most of the wares sold in Chinese shops were becoming familiar to me, but many of these shops had a few odd and beautiful pieces of something or other that was not usual. In Black Wood Street were furniture and porcelain shops; the air was filled with the smell of freshly cut woods, sandalwood and teak for example, and furniture polish and banana oil. Farther on metal workers hammered on brass, or fashioned items such as candlesticks, plates, locks, or water pipes of silver or copper. The porcelain and china wares for sale were some of the best I had seen thus far in China, with clean, straight lines, and colors that ranged from light pastel shades to dark, rich reds, browns and greens.

One street specialized in firecrackers, another in dry goods and materials, and in the street where the rice merchants had their shops beggars collected to sweep up grains fallen to the ground. It was obvious these people depended on their sweepings to survive, and it was dismaying to see people surviving at this level of existence. One could easily imagine robbery and murder as a logical step up for anyone who had fallen so far on the human scale.

And that step up was not far away, for in one little nearby shop, an outlet for smuggled goods, all the things available in Hong Kong (canned goods, liquor, foreign beer) were available at reasonable prices. Smuggling and piracy were booming businesses in south China. Sources for goods were close by in Hong Kong and Macao, and ways to get them into China were simple, various and relatively risk-free. Money to back the smuggling rings was said to come from overseas Chinese because, with most dealings done in Hong Kong dollars, this offered a very attractive investment outlet for them.

The streets themselves were wonderful, many so narrow that nothing on wheels could pass through them. Banners hung from the upper stories of the buildings facing these lanes, and sometimes awnings stretched across the passageway between opposing buildings. Sun filtered through these awnings, casting interesting shadows and patterns on the cobblestones and large stone blocks that served as paving. At intervals other little streets cut into or across these lanes, all hopelessly clogged with wares, buyers and sellers, laundry, cooking fires, dogs, and babies. Everywhere you looked life stirred, crawled, hopped, walked, ran, pushed, shoved and breathed.

Another happy surprise was the Watsons, the Stanvac district manager and his wife. Bill Watson was about forty at the time, medium height but with a fairly trim figure, and balding in a way that left a little tuft of hair on the front of his scalp, reminding me of the old comic strip character of Foxy Grandpa. Bill was always smiling, and his manner was relaxed, gracious and attentive. When he asked someone to do something, his manner changed to a state of near-embarrassment, as though he could not bear to ask anything that might take up your time or burden you in any way. He never ordered anything directly, but asked politely as though it were a favor he sought, or a suggestion that something be done. No one minded getting directions like these, and his way of issuing them insured they would be carried out promptly.

Both Bill and his wife, whose name was Elizabeth but was called simply "E," were from Virginia; they had married in Hong Kong only a year earlier. They made a great couple, and shared an enormous interest in everything Chinese. They loved to explore the city's streets, its shops and the surrounding countryside, and had furnished their apartment with many tasteful and lovely Chinese objects. "E" had an outgoing personality, enjoyed a laugh and good conversation, read a lot, got a terrific kick out of living, and did everything with great enthusiasm. She made me feel welcome in Canton with a naturalness and warmth rare to find anywhere.

Bill won my attention and respect almost from the start when he commented disgustedly one day, in the course of some conversation or other, on people stationed in Canton who bragged that the only time they left Shameen was to catch the river boat for Hong Kong. To make a comment like that he obviously was not just another thirty-year company man, sitting out his term until retirement.

He liked where he was, had a wide circle of Chinese friends, and and was making the most of his opportunity to live and work in China. I liked the Watsons immediately, and felt most grateful that Bill would be my first Stanvac manager.

First impressions of some of the other foreign staff were less favorable, excluding Ron who had yet to appear. The assistant manager was an accountant by training, who had arrived in Canton only three days before I did. He and his wife were therefore also new and in the process of settling in. Both were quite tall, and he struck me as phlegmatic, dull even, the way I imagined all accountants to be. He subsequently turned out to be stubborn and opinionated as well. His wife seemed pleasant and more open, but had an unfortunate breathless way of talking that made her gush about everything.

A second couple were the Petersons, "Pete" and Edna, who lived in the apartment above mine. He joined Stanvac in the same batch that included Neil MacFadyen, and had been in China only a little more than a year. Pete was short and blond, with eyes that seemed continually red-rimmed (I learned later that he suffered from trachoma), and wore a preoccupied air that never left him. Originally from New Jersey, he had been a pilot during the war, liked to drink and gamble, and fit the description Lyn had given me of the bored, "macho" pilots and air crew members she had met her first few months in Peip'ing. Pete was a "company man" in all respects. He liked the work and seemed to have no doubts he would make his career with the company. He had an uncle who was general manager at the time in Indochina, so family influences probably contributed to his attitudes about where he was and what the future held for him.

Edna Peterson was from Brooklyn, and still had traces of the accent from there. They had one child already, a girl about three or four years old named Karen, and were expecting a second fairly soon. The Petersons were very good to me on my arrival, inviting me up to their apartment for dinner and doing their best to orient me to the new post. Unfortunately, from my point of view, they had a standard, insular, foreigner-in-China attitude toward most things, and the orientation they offered was essentially how to minimize the China experience and never leave home. They confined their interests to a small social circle, worried they might not have ample supplies on hand of imported articles and provisions, and became involved with things Chinese as little as possible. I certainly did not dislike the Petersons, and was genuinely grateful for the assistance they offered and the interest they showed in me, but on first impressions I did not expect a close friendship to develop.

The Stanvac "family" in Canton included two other couples. One of these lived above us in the same apartment building. The man was the chief accountant for the Canton office, quiet and preoccupied with financial matters, and I saw relatively little of him and his wife. The other couple was the Suters. He was a Swiss national, in charge of the terminal where the petroleum products were landed and stored. His wife was Canadian, pretty and extremely nice. I soon learned, by inference rather than by being told, that people who work at the terminals were lesser breeds, above Chinese in social status but below those of us who worked, for example, in the "front office." This became evident when the Suters did not appear at the dinners and cocktail parties that were almost daily features, and where the same small group of foreigners from Stanvac, Shell, other businesses and the diplomatic community was always included.

After a week or so at work I was still not clear about what I would be doing as a Stanvac employee. I was told to "read the files," and tried to grasp the terms, abbreviations and figures as they went by. After spending a few days on this I still had only a dim understanding of what the business was all about. A second bit of training/orientation was to take inventories of stock, which consisted of counting drums of gasoline, kerosene and oil, and making entries on huge sheets of paper printed for the purpose. The company had a very accurate count of everything already, but it was probably a time-honored custom to assign new people to "take inventory," something done to help them "get a feel for things."

The stocks I was counting were in the storage terminal, and to get there I would leave the house early in the morning and take a company launch a short distance down the river. On those Fall mornings, as the sun was rising over the city, all the river people would be stirring, cooking fires were going, and the sampan dwellers were getting ready for the day. The night boat from Hong Kong would be just coming up the river, a big, white, snub-nosed vessel that looked the way I imagined packet boats on the Mississippi once looked. This was all very new and colorful to me, and it made the trip down to the installation, by itself, almost worth the monotony of counting oil drums all day.

The scene when junks were being loaded for up-country shipments also fascinated me. As I wrote to Lyn, "The oil may have started in Arabia, travelled halfway across the world to the U.S. to be put through a series of Rube Goldberg products, the most modern that science can devise, and so become useful articles. Then back across the world in modern tankers to finally be loaded by coolies onto river boats that are much like those used five hundred years ago. The coolies chant as they lift the drums aboard — it is a syncopated rhythm that one shouts and the other answers — so they keep in step to the beat of the chant. As they pass a man sitting by the gangplank they pick up a stick, and at the end of the day are paid by the number of sticks they have. I do not see how they do it, but with a heave the drums are up, and they trot off laughing and joking as they go down to the boats. And in some up-country village the long trip ends, and the oil burns in some farmer's lamp...It's the last step in what would make a good story... the daily lives of people who handled one particular batch of oil from the field to the consumer — Arabs, engineers, British sea captains, Indian crews, American refinery employees, shippers, salesmen, Chinese agents, coolies, and the consumer —and what happened to each on the day he came in contact with this particular shipment."

In addition to taking inventory and reading files, another early assignment was to figure out the most economic routing for trucks delivering gasoline to Stanvac service stations throughout the Canton area. I plugged away at this for a while, but kept overlooking things that affected the viability of the schedule, such as the drivers' days off, or the fact that one truck can carry only so many gallons per trip. This was part of a familiarization process prior to taking on responsibility for supervising service station operations in the city. Eventually a delivery schedule of sorts did emerge from my efforts, but I doubt it was much of an improvement over what it replaced.

I remember feeling sorry for Bill Watson at the time, overworked and inundated by company brass from Shanghai and Hong Kong making inspection trips to the Canton office. He must have prayed for an addition to his staff of someone with engineering background or experience, someone able to jump right in and help him with some of the knotty problems he faced. Instead, he got a totally green hand in me, who had to be assigned to routine and largely meaningless tasks, such as taking inventory, to keep me from getting in the way.

While all this was going on, it had become very clear that Lyn's and my summer romance was not fleeting, but a very serious thing. I missed her greatly, and

61

was writing letters at the rate of four or more a week. Writing became a way to spend time together, an opportunity I grabbed every chance I had. I even resented being invited out, because that cut into my writing time. Not only did I try to share with Lyn my own impressions and experiences in the new surroundings, but I also poured out thoughts on books I had read, the China military/political situation, views on poetry, what the future might hold, religion and philosophy, and anything else that came to mind that I thought would interest Lyn. And, of course, there was a great deal about missing her, wanting to be with her, and recalling the times we had together in Peip'ing. For someone who had never written very often to anyone before, and who generally found correspondence a dull, though sometimes necessary, chore, I was amazed at how easy it was to maintain the steady flow of letters. Lyn responded to my letters as faithfully as I sent them. The subject of marriage came up with increasing frequency in this correspondence, and that started very quickly after I had reached Canton.

The discussion of marriage was usually in the context of three options we saw looming ahead: the first was that Lyn would return to the U.S. alone and wait for my three-year assignment to end; the second was to wait and see whether Stanvac would change its policy toward first-term marriage; and the third was to drop everything and either get married in Canton, or both of us return to the U.S. and be married there as soon as we could arrange things. The central option seemed the wisest and most prudent, and that was our focus. But we had crossed a major threshold in our thinking. The resolve to be hard headed and objective about the frailty of summer romances disappeared, and we became definite in our minds that marriage was somewhere in the offing for us.

Peip'ing, Fall 1947

As the Fall Term got underway at PAS, there was good news and bad news. The good news was the new household arrangements were working out very well. Lyn liked Dorie and the Scott sisters, and they were pleased Lyn had joined them. The compound where they lived was spacious and comfortable, and not too far from places in the city they might want to visit. They were also fortunate to have two congenial and capable servants to look after their needs: a man named T'ien who was the cook, and his wife "Martha" (Chinese name never given) who was the housekeeper and laundress. Martha spoke no English, and had a very limited conversational range even in kitchen Chinese, but she and T'ien were nice people and took good care of the household. All in all, living in Fang Chia Yuan turned out to be as satisfactory as one could wish.

The bad news was that life at school was not pleasant. Ruth was now acting as the principal, and in many little ways she was making Lyn's situation as disagreeable as possible. Lyn's departure from the old compound continued to rankle Ruth, as did the knowledge that Lyn had been everyone's first choice to serve as acting principal. So, there were days when Ruth chose not to speak, or messages would somehow not be passed on to Lyn. I stopped addressing letters to Lyn at the school for fear they might not be delivered to her. If something in the school had to be done, yet was onerous for some reason, or time-consuming, Lyn would get the assignment. The classes, on the other hand, were fine. Lyn's rapport with students was as strong as ever, and she liked working with many of the other members of the faculty. The sour note came solely from the petty, spiteful, harassing incidents that emanated from Ruth, now in a position of some authority over Lyn.

There was another bit of unpleasantness. The head of the PAS school board, Ernest Shaw, came to Lyn with a disturbing story one day toward the end of October. Dr. Shaw was a kindly person, a member of the American Board Mission in Peip'ing, the father of the Lee Shaw who had originally encouraged Lyn to go to China, and the uncle of Gen Shaw. Because of the latter relationship, we often referred to him as "Uncle Ernest," though not to his face. He had, however, taken an avuncular interest in Lyn from the start, had been impressed with the job she had done at the school, and had wanted her to take the job of acting principal.

The news he presented to Lyn was that three of the missionary wives in town had been saying openly that Lyn was not fit to be a teacher at PAS. They alleged she was promiscuous with men, appeared frequently in public in an intoxicated condition, and generally carried on in an unladylike manner. A fourth wife brought these allegations to Ernest Shaw, not that she shared them but because she thought the head of the school board should know about them. Ernest did not accept the charges at face value, and was generally supportive when he talked with Lyn, but he was firm in advising her that the gossip was serious and something needed to be done about it. Lyn was, expectedly, shaken by this turn of events, but acted promptly by inviting the four ladies to tea one afternoon. All appeared at the compound at the appointed time, and when they were seated Lyn faced them and said:

"I am not going to serve you tea, though I admit inviting you for that purpose, because sharing refreshments together implies that a friendly relationship exists. That is not true in this case. I have been told you have been spreading malicious and untrue stories about my behavior, although I do not know on what basis you know me or can say anything about me. None of you has ever invited me into her home for dinner, tea, or for any reason at all. You have never consulted me about your children's progress in school. None of you have attended any school function when I was either the teacher responsible or was a participating faculty member. How can you know what sort of person I am, other than through hearsay?

"I believe none of you know that I am the eldest of a family of six children that includes an adopted brother and sister, that my father is a distinguished professor at a major U.S. university, and that my academic achievements and personal life have always been above reproach. You are nevertheless prepared to attack my reputation by repeating irresponsible gossip. If you have any questions about what I do or what sort of person I am, please ask them now so I may answer them directly. Otherwise, please refrain from spreading harmful stories about me in the future."

The ladies sat in shocked silence for a minute or two, but the room soon came alive with the buzz of denial and backtracking. They would not repeat malicious stories, they were quick to say, although it was true they had not been very hospitable to a young woman who had come into their community to teach their children. In fact, they said, their children kept telling them what a wonderful teacher Miss Kreps was, how interesting her classes were, and how much they learned in them. The air was suddenly full of Lyn's praises, and with the ladies' remonstrances that no criticism was intended in anything they may have said. No, they continued, everyone felt the school had been most fortunate to hire Lyn to teach in a foreign country, among strangers, under difficult conditions, and it was widely agreed she was doing an outstanding job.

After a certain amount of this it was evident tea really was not about to appear, and the ladies were left with no choice but to gather their effects and make a polite withdrawal.

The matter of Lyn's deportment was never raised again. Where the stories started, and what fueled them, was never known, but the suspicion was always strong in our minds that Ruth had somehow been behind the whole incident. At about this time, too, Lyn began to express in her letters a sense of discouragement about school and being in Peip'ing, and raised more than once the possibility of walking away from all the unpleasantness and going back to Palo Alto.

When I was getting ready to transfer to Canton, Lyn and I had agreed that we should feel free to date others as we wished because there was no commitment between us. Lyn was finding this easier to do than I did. Peip'ing was now well supplied with single young people, and Neil MacFadyen was making certain Lyn promptly met the new batch of Stanvac classmen who had come for language training. Neil's continuing strategy was to dissuade us from getting too serious about each other, and this meant he now made certain Lyn had some alternative attractions.

He really did not have to work too hard at it, though. There were plenty of parties and outings that Fall and Lyn, along with Dorie and the Scott sisters, was always included. The compound at Fang Chia Yuan was, in fact, an active center in this social scene, with dinners, parties and impromptu gatherings taking place more or less continuously. However socially active Lyn's life was, it did not dampen or delay the flow of her letters from Peip'ing to Canton. This was a mixed blessing for me because hearing from Lyn had become an important part of my life, but I did not relish hearing about all the new young men she was meeting.

Lyn and Lee Bomberger in
traditional Chinese costume

Lyn mailing letter to Canton

Lyn, Dorie Eldred and Scott sisters with
T'ien, the cook at Fang Chia Yuan

Group photo of contemporaries

CHAPTER SEVEN

> PIRATES IN CHINA SEA KIDNAP SIX FROM SHIP
>
> New York Times, December 16,1947, p. 30.
>
> COMMUNISTS CUT 3 PEIP'ING LINES TO TIGHTEN BLOCKADE OF MUKDEN
>
> New York Times, December 30, 1947, p. 11.

Canton, Late Fall 1947

My new mess-mate, Ron Carey, returned from his field trip toward the end of October. Ron was born in China, son of one of the early telephone pioneers in China who had represented several American telephone equipment companies. Ron spoke fluent Chinese, was a graduate of the Shanghai American School and the University of Pennsylvania, and at 23 was somewhat younger than the other classmen. I found him likable, easy-going and friendly, and we got along well from the start.

Ron's trip up-country was an eye-opener to what working for Stanvac might entail. By his account he had slept in bandit strongholds, traveled through some former head-hunting territory, rode Chinese junks up the river and slept on kerosene drums while on board to keep the drums from being stolen, had eaten rice to the point of satiety, but had been flea-bitten only once. This sounded pretty exciting and interesting to me, particularly since he had come through it all without harmful effects.

At about this same time I heard about a possible Stanvac initiative that might concern me in the near future. The company had been experiencing long delays in getting supplies of gasoline, oil and kerosene into the western portion of the

Canton district, i.e., the area served through the city of K'unming. The supplies were taking as long as six months to reach their destination, not only a costly procedure but also opportunity for strange things to happen to the products en route. Some of the Shanghai Stanvac executives were toying with the idea of running a Stanvac trucking fleet from Liuchow, a city at the uppermost navigable reaches of the West River. Petroleum products would be shipped that far by boat and there transferred into trucks for a thousand kilometer haul over the mountains to K'unming. The headquarters for this operation would be in the city of Kweiyang, roughly the halfway point of the proposed truck route and about 200 miles south of Chungking. There would be one foreigner managing this trucking venture, the rest of the staff being Chinese, and I would probably be that manager if the proposal were actually accepted. The posting to Kweiyang would be for only six months at a time however, to minimize the stress on the manager and keep him sane. For some odd and illogical reason this sounded fascinating to me, even though the problems would be superhuman — accidents, robberies, fire, breakdowns, maintenance problems, and continual worry whether the trucks were getting through.

By mid-October I was also well into the socialization process, and learning what life in a small foreign community could be like. It was considered proper in Canton at the time for newcomers to make formal "calls" on established residents. You dropped a calling card if no one was at home, or stayed to chat a bit if invited in to do so. This seemed very British to me, and a little awkward since I did not really know the rules of the game, but nevertheless I set out one afternoon on my social duties. My first stop was the home of the U.S. Naval Attaché, and I had such an interesting time talking and drinking Manhattans with the Attaché and his wife that I made no farther progress on my rounds that day. The Attaché was born in Japan, so we conversed for a while in Japanese, traded pleasantries on the beauties of Japan, and generally enjoyed ourselves while the hour grew late.

Despite this promising start, "E" Watson recognized I was basically reluctant to drop in on people I had never seen before. Believing strongly I should complete my rounds nevertheless, she volunteered to accompany me on the other "calls" on my list. With her amiable assistance, I managed to meet the requisite number of senior people in residence in due course, and thereby officially "arrived" on post.

A China Story: From Peip'ing to Beijing

Another part of the social life was athletics, and I was quickly enlisted to play first base on the Shameen resident softball team. Our opponents were a team made up of men who worked with Civil Air Transport (CAT), the private freight and passenger airline owned by Gen. Chennault and staffed largely with men who had flown in China with his "Flying Tigers" during WW II. These were mostly healthy young "fly boys," whereas our team ranged in age from myself to the American Consul General, a gentleman of at least 55 summers, and with a preponderance of the balding and stout among us. We usually managed to beat the CAT team, somehow, despite the other team's obvious physical advantages. Tennis, rowing and riding were also available, though tennis was the only one on which I spent any time.

Farther down on a scale of strenuousness were billiards or snooker at the Canton Club, neither one of which I played well. Aside from these two games of skill, and a few tired magazines, the Canton Club offered little in the way of entertainment save beer and lethal "pink gins" [gin with a dash of bitters and no ice]. Standard Saturday afternoon procedure (everyone worked Saturday mornings) was to assemble at the Canton Club for snooker and several pink gins, followed by a large curry lunch and an afternoon nap that took us until the evening. The captain of one of the Hong Kong/Canton river boats was a snooker player of some accomplishment, which probably reflected the amount of time he spent at snooker when not on the river. He never failed to blast his boat's whistle as he passed the club, hoping to startle one of his cronies into a bad shot in the process.

Dinner parties were a continuing, very frequent social feature because people could not think of many other ways to entertain each other. As time passed the parties grew less and less appealing to me because of the constant repetition of party behavior. The party format was pretty rigidly fixed — drinks at the start, dinner of four or five courses, then bridge and more drinks to round out the evening. Conversation was predictable, running heavily to gossip about the foreign community, troubles with servants, places to get bargains in Hong Kong, and what people planned to do on their next home leave. Exceptions to this were dinner parties at the Watsons, where topics of some substance were discussed and actual ideas bandied about.

And finally, least active of all the sports were the stag poker or crap games that were regular features on at least one or two nights of any week. Pete was an avid organizer of these, but he was not alone in his enthusiasm. My participation in these was more out of a sense of wanting to appear a "good guy" than having any relish for gambling. I played conservatively, which meant that I lost more often than I won, but never lost a great deal. On occasion, someone would lose more than he could really afford, and this was painful to watch. A card game called "Red Dog" was particularly vicious in this respect because each player bet against the pot for any amount he wished, up to the size of the pot itself. Winning or losing depended on the turn of a card. This could mean serious losses when several players in a row failed to win and the pot, if matched, was very large.

These were grown men, and if they wanted to take big risks that was their business, but as a I wrote to Lyn about one such session, "... embarrassed minutes of silence fall over the table, and the loser gets that queer, sick look in his eyes that shows he knows he has gone too far, though he tries to carry things off as well as he can. This leaves me with the feeling I get when a singer hits a bad note at a concert, or an actor forgets his lines — it's uncomfortable and I'm sorry when I have to see it."

Gradually, by fits and starts, Ron Carey and I managed to get some furnishings for the apartment. Nothing came easily, and drapes in particular had to be sent back a few times before they fit, but finally the apartment lost its rough edges and began to look and feel more comfortable. I designed and commissioned a piece of furniture to house my phonograph and records and books, but when it appeared the thing looked more like a packing box, which it basically was, than a proper console.

Ron and I attacked the furnishing problem without much help from Ah Tung, the cook/servant who came with the apartment. Ah Tung was the perfect model of Asian inscrutability. I described him to Lyn as "...a stone-faced, stoic, unmovable Chinese with no emotion within him at all...his only expression was a sort of quizzical, half-understanding, vaguely unhappy look that has never changed while I could see it. There seem to be no extremes in his life — no love or hate, fear or courage, black or white, right or wrong. He just does what he is told, offers no comments, expresses no ideas, gives no suggestions — and, I think, sleeps when he's not cooking or serving ...You always have to provide the spark because his imagination seems non-existent. At first he annoyed me, but now I am used to him, and almost like him — but I don't understand him."

The socializing, sports and on-the-job training all came to an abrupt halt, though. On a Thursday evening, end of October, I had dinner at the Peterson's, but left early. Early Friday morning I awoke with a gnawing feeling in my stomach, not helped at all by a couple of bad eggs for breakfast. By evening this had definitely become a stomach ache of major proportions. I went to bed early again, but not to sleep much, and early Saturday morning hauled myself to the foot bridge that led to the mainland and hailed a pedicab to take me to the Presbyterian Mission Hospital.

After trying to explain my symptoms at the reception desk, I was directed to a room on the second floor and almost before I realized what was happening found myself on an operating table and being given a local anesthetic. This was my first local. The imagination runs mightily because you can feel the surgeon at work, tugging, cutting and sewing, even though there is no pain. The Chinese doctor who operated was very good, and the whole thing was over rather quickly and with a minimum of chit chat.

When the doctor had finished there was a knock at the door of the operating room and in walked Ron and Pete, Ron with a letter from Lyn in hand. They had come to find out what had happened to me, were simply told where to find me upstairs, but were not told that an operation was in progress. Their faces registered considerable shock when the doctor welcomed them in, assured them that the operation had been successful, and held out for their inspection the appendix he had just removed from me. I waved a weak greeting from the operating table, and they mumbled something in return, but the circumstances were so bizarre they were not disposed to linger and talk and quickly withdrew.

After they left, and all the post-operative chores were completed, four coolie women came in with a stretcher and loaded me aboard with much bustle and jostling. Together, we set off at a fast trot for the room where I would convalesce. To them the task seemed a huge joke, and they laughed and enjoyed it, especially going down the stairs. My bottom bumped a little on the risers because the ladies were so short, and the weight of my body in the canvas stretcher created a protuberance that did not quite clear the stairs as we went down. This sent them into peals of glee, and the comedy aspect continued when the nurses, who spoke no English, tried to converse with me once I had been deposited in my room.

Barnyard humor was the order of the day. I spoke no Cantonese, and when I tried to reply to them in Mandarin, or communicate with gestures, they just giggled and ran from the room. Each nurse had some little duty to perform: one filled the water pitcher, one bathed me, one took down and hung up the mosquito netting, one handled bedpans and such, and another took pulses and temperatures. This resulted in a steady stream of people coming into the room at certain times of the day, and with them much embarrassed giggling.

The interns' knowledge of English was almost as limited as the nurses', and when they tried to write down my case history the results were highly unsatisfactory. The interns did not seem to understand what I told them, not helped by the fact I did not understand much of what they were asking, and there were lots of "how's thats?" and "whats?" on both sides. Their case history forms, as far as I could tell, were as blank when they left as when they came in. Just outside my window was a middle school, from which the din of lesson recitations, sports, calisthenics and drilling floated through my open window most of each day. I also discovered that I was in the maternity section, confirmed by the nearby sound of small babies being taken to or from their mothers, and I was the only male there.

The hospital was part of the Presbyterian Mission in Canton, and despite my antipathy toward missionary activities in general I was very glad this mission was there when I needed it. I was afraid at first that a prayer committee would visit and insist that I do something about my Sabbath devotions, but none did and I was left alone in that respect. The hospital was on the dingy side, as was much of everything else in China, but ample medical supplies were on hand and the staff doctors were very capable. The entire hospital was in Chinese hands, except for a few Americans who served as administrators, which explains my communications problems with the staff. Bill Watson offered to charter a plane to take me to Hong Kong if I wanted that, but I felt quite content and secure where I was and declined his kind, and expensive, offer.

My recovery was rapid and free of complications. A few days on a liquid diet left me with cravings for sardines, anchovies, shrimp, lamb chops and turkey, all unavailable in a mission hospital, and I lost some weight. By mid-week I was up and around a little and anxious to return to the apartment. People were very kind to me, and I had multiple visitors daily. I was particularly flattered to receive a visit from Mr. Seong, the most senior Chinese in the Stanvac office. He was a fine old gentleman, highly respected in Canton, and a good friend of the doctor who had operated on me. "E" Watson also visited regularly and kept me supplied with books and the exotic foods I missed. At one point she and Mrs. Goodspeed, wife of one of the Stanavac staff, decided I needed a bed lamp to read by, and made arrangements to bring me one. This turned out to be quite a comic exercise.

On the first try "E" forgot to bring both the lamp and Mrs. Goodspeed, so had to return for them, in some embarrassment. Next, the good ladies had forgotten to check the voltage in the hospital, and on the first try promptly blew out the bulb. This meant another trip for more bulbs, but the driver of the company car had misunderstood their instructions to wait and returned to the hospital to pick up Ron and Pete, who had meanwhile come in another car to visit me. After about 45 minutes of their visit had passed, Pete noticed the driver seemed to be waiting for them and checked to see what was going on. Once he understood the mix-up, he quickly dispatched the driver back to pick up the stranded ladies. They finally returned with the bulbs, and in a boiling rage at being left waiting. When Mrs. Goodspeed tried to put in the first bulb it gave her such a shock she dropped the bulb on the floor with a loud "pop!" Five minutes later, after getting up enough nerve to put in the spare she had brought, the bulb worked like a charm. At that point Mrs. Goodspeed spotted an elderly Chinese woman in the corridor, watching all this with some amazement. When she ordered her to clean up the broken glass the lady, who was a patient and not a charwoman, merely smiled and moved on.

After a week, my stitches removed and feeling quite chipper except for occasional twinges here and there, I was ready to leave the hospital. Bill Watson had laid on arrangements to minimize physical strain for me on the return trip, including coolies to lift me up the steps of the footbridge and a rickshaw to carry me tenderly the three blocks from bridge to the apartment. In the van of the procession on that final leg came the coolies, carrying the books, bed lamp, fruit and other odds and ends I had collected during the week past; I followed riding in the faded splendor of a rickshaw, lacking crown and ermine robe but feeling slightly regal nevertheless.

Back in the apartment, where I had been ordered to stay for another week's convalescence, I enjoyed the luxury of whole days to myself. I sunned myself on the verandah, wrote long letters to Lyn, entertained a continuing stream of visitors, slept late, and began moving about on short walks in the neighborhood. A few days of this was enough, however, and I became bored and anxious to be back on a normal routine.

This was also the time plans were beginning to gel for Lyn to visit Canton over the Christmas/New Year holiday. I was delighted she would be willing to make the trip, and pleased to hear that Dorie and the Scott sisters had endorsed the idea. I wrote Lyn that I planned to tell people she was my fiancée, though we were not actually engaged, because that put a more "respectable" face on things than introducing her as simply a friend from Peip'ing. I was also concerned she might find Canton less interesting than Peip'ing because the social life was rather dull, and I would be at work during the daytime every day but Christmas and New Year's. That would leave her in the hands of others for things to do, but maybe "E" Watson would take over and show her around a bit. The only hotel on Shameen did not enjoy a good reputation for comfort or cleanliness, so Ron stepped in and made initial arrangements for Lyn to stay with one of the British secretaries in the Shell office.

The marriage issue was coming very much alive in company circles at that point, and beginning to move slowly toward some kind of resolution. Nate Zimmerman, who had been engaged before coming to China, wrote that he discussed Stanvac's no-marriage policy with the assistant general manager when that gentleman was in Hong Kong on a recent business visit. Nate told him he wanted to get married sometime during the coming year because he, Nate, had been told when hired that a year to a year and a half would be all the time he would probably have to wait. Nate added he did not intend to rush matters, but the opportunity to raise the issue seemed too good to pass up. The assistant general manager told Nate he would talk the matter over with the general manager and let Nate know the outcome, but at least did not reject outright the idea of marriage. I was pleased to see Nate taking the lead, since some kind of commitment had apparently been made in his case before he left for China, and I felt if a precedent could be set by someone else it might be easier for us to make our case.

A China Story: From Peip'ing to Beijing

On the other hand, my feelings had reached a stage where staying with the company was no longer a keystone in my thinking about the future. As I wrote to Lyn, "...the [Stanvac] job is a factor to consider, but it isn't the most important one. Life is not always worth living if you make a 'smart' decision. I know I would be more miserable waiting three long years [to marry] than would ever be repaid in money, security, or ease in living [over] any number of years to come. We're not so unintelligent, ungifted or unlucky that we can't make a new start if we have to do so."

This attitude was not just the result of our being apart; other factors were at work. In another letter about the same time I wrote: "And while we're on the subject of the COMPANY — I'm really getting to hate that word — the trucking idea has fallen through, and I won't be getting an assignment that looked most interesting. To get back to that word — COMPANY — every time I use it I feel as though I'm bound over to it, body and soul. In some quarters, the word is used with awe and reverence, and I think some of the old Chinese employees think of Stanvac as a deity of some sort, one that makes no mistakes and does no wrong. It's like the army in lots of ways; the COMPANY wraps you up, and being in a country like China people working for it lean heavily on it for support. It's a pretty natural step, but it seems that every other sentence contains the COMPANY this, the COMPANY that, and always the tone implies the capital letters...I think it's mighty grand to be enthusiastic about your job and to like and admire the company you work for, and I wouldn't want it otherwise, but I don't quite buy the near-reverence with which the older men seem to regard the COMPANY."

A week after leaving the hospital I was back in the office, actually glad to have something to do and ready to resume life on more or less normal terms. My twenty-sixth birthday came and went without much fanfare, and I learned a business trip to Hong Kong was scheduled for me a week later. The river boats between Hong Kong and Canton had begun running only in the daytime because a Chinese vessel had been blown up by a mine in the river. The Chinese boat had refused to pay a bribe of HK$ 100,000 to river pirates, and it was generally believed that pirates had been responsible for the mine. In another incident, a Stanvac agent had his junk pirated and all his stock taken. The area around Canton had become a smuggler's paradise, as noted earlier, with large amounts of contraband flowing into China from Hong Kong and Macao, and pirates were now actively raiding the smugglers as well as normal river traffic. Unlike North China, where Communist forces were gaining strength and extending their areas of control, there was no Communist military presence in the south. Pirates and bandits were becoming an extremely serious problem, though, and because of them communication by either land or water had become hazardous.

To add fuel to my already burgeoning preoccupation with getting married, another couple's wedding was to be held in Canton the Saturday before I was due to leave for Hong Kong. The groom was a young Shell classman, Ron Malcolm. Although Shell had the same general rules as Stanvac with respect to marriage, Ron had received permission to bring his bride-to-be from Scotland, and to be married before his initial overseas tour was completed. I do not recall the grounds for this dispensation, but the fact he had received one indicated that company policies need not be forever rigid, and that in itself was encouraging.

The day of the wedding was bright and sunny, with a cool breeze that made it perfect for the occasion. The site was the small Anglican church on Shameen, only a few doors from my apartment, and the guest list included most of the foreign community. The setting was lovely by any standard, but to my critical eye the ceremony fell short of expectations. For one thing, the church organ was wheezy and weak, and the man playing it had not practiced enough to get the hymns and processionals right. For another, many of the guests arrived late, as though the wedding were a cocktail party. The late-comers were not quiet about it, either. Finally, the Anglican ceremony was unnecessarily long for my taste. Perhaps the Malcolms felt so as well, because Ron practically ran down the aisle pulling Janet along with him when the ceremony was over. In any case, I liked Ron Malcolm and wished him and his new bride well, but my summary comment on the wedding to Lyn was, "Let's not get married in Canton!"

I was looking forward to the Hong Kong trip, but not because it might be fun to pick out lubricating tools and equipment for the Canton service stations (the purpose of the trip). Rather, I wanted a chance to talk with Nate about his dialogue with company officials over marriage policy. I was also hoping to add some phonograph records to my meager stock, get an Australian beef steak dinner (instead of water buffalo), some good ice cream, and a milk shake.

A China Story: From Peip'ing to Beijing

There had been speculation that the British company running the Hong Kong/Canton river service would suspend operations until the river pirates could be cleared out, but at the time boats were still providing daytime service. This was a very pleasant way to travel. The boats were large, fat, shallow draft vessels equipped with bars, dining rooms, lounges, deck chairs and all sorts of little comforts. Like the coastal vessel I had taken from T'ientsin, river boats also had armed guards and protective steel grills to seal off the wheelhouse and first class portions of the ship in the event of an attack.

The river trip was a wonderful scenic experience, and I described the countryside to Lyn in glowing terms: "...so peaceful and calm, all green and brown with mountains for a background and clear blue skies...in surroundings as lovely as these, life may be hard, but it must also be rewarding in ways other than money returns and physical possessions." One could understand why traditional Chinese poets and artists had gone to the country for inspiration, and "...the country must be the same today. There has not been much change; the fields are as green, the mountains and sky are constant things, the houses and temples are as they were then, and life is much the same. One can see why they could find all this such a wonderful place, and why they could believe China was the "Middle Kingdom.' To them, China was the focal point of the earth — no other place could be lovelier."

As the boat neared Hong Kong, the river became wider at its mouth, the fields pretty much disappeared, mountains came right down to the river's edge, and there were many small islands. As in North China, the mountains had long since been stripped of trees, if ever there were any, leaving them brown and barren. Fishing boats were plentiful, but towns were widely scattered along the shore.

The Hong Kong stay went pretty much as expected. A steak dinner came right away, followed by a double chocolate sundae, and since the Watsons were also there on vacation there was a chance to have coffee with "E" and bring her up to date on Canton gossip. They had missed the Malcolm wedding, for example. There was also some talk about a transfer to Hong Kong, but it turned out this was based on the assumption I was an expert on lubricating oil. Since I knew nothing about lubricating oil, and was very happy watching people paint gas stations in Canton, Bill said he would scratch the transfer possibility.

The update from Nate Zimmerman had not changed much. Talks with managers had been encouraging, but nothing definite was said by anyone. Talking with Nate was an easy way to work ourselves into a nice pessimistic, gloomy mood. An optimistic attitude came hard in Hong Kong. The hustle and bustle of the place made things seem colder and more business-like, as it did in Shanghai. Optimism somehow came more naturally in sleepy old Canton.

By the end of the week the equipment was in hand, along with the information needed to install it properly, and it was time to leave. There was time for a bit of shopping, mostly Christmas cards and presents bought at the request of others in Canton, and a final dinner at the Peninsula Hotel with Nate. Though we were poor company for each other, it was Thanksgiving. Some small celebration seemed in order, but the hotel's turkey proved disappointing.

The next day, back on the river heading for Canton and sitting on deck in the warm sunshine writing to Lyn, I had just finished describing the beauty of the sunrise over the harbor in Hong Kong that morning, all gold and red. After breaking off for a bite to eat, the letter went on:

"Just after lunch, about fifteen minutes ago, while standing at the rail and smoking a cigarette, a Customs launch came speeding up and a couple of [uniformed] men from it came aboard. The launch followed alongside but suddenly, from another boat [astern from us] that looked like a landing craft, there came shots. Men still in the Customs launch replied to this with rifles and machine gun fire, and for a minute it looked like a running battle. But the boat in the rear dropped back, the firing stopped, and the whole thing was over almost as soon as it started. Some Customs men are still aboard, and the launch is following, but no one seems to know what happened, or why. This boat has been found carrying smuggled goods before. Something similar may be aboard now and the Customs people, having received a tip, may have come aboard to check things out. The other boat may be part of the gang who was supposed to get the stuff, and were trying to move in and scare off the Customs officers. Piracy and smuggling are so common that almost everyone either engages in them actively or helps by buying the stuff they bring in...The big item smuggled in lately has been dyestuffs for use in the textile mills in Canton, and of course luxury goods of all kinds are brought in, too. There doesn't seem much the government can do about it. Even if the Customs were free of corruption, which is probably not the case, there are too many ways to smuggle and too many people involved...Little shootings like this will go on, and so will the smuggling; everyone will urge that incidents like this be stopped, but I doubt anyone can come up with a solution that might solve the mess."

Once the excitement was over, and the Customs officers were back on their launch and drifting away from us, we continued without incident to Canton. The usual office and social routines returned quickly, but a day later there was news that put a totally different twist to my story. According to this latest information, the Customs launch was really a pirate boat, and the supposed pirate boat [astern of us] was really a Customs vessel. The pirates who came from the launch, uniforms and all, had come aboard amidships, and were starting to commandeer our boat when the shooting started and drove them away.

The man who had this news said we passengers were lucky to still have our valuables, because the pirates had been ready to go after the passengers when the Customs boat appeared! As I sat at a dinner party that evening, people talking and laughing around me, things proceeding normally, everyone free of worry and behaving in the usual way, I wondered whether this was really the top of some volcano. When will it blow? Is this just like Shanghai and Hong Kong in 1941, when people like my dinner partners refused to believe the Japanese were serious? Are we kidding ourselves? We may be too close to the whole thing to see what's actually happening, but there seems little we can do about it. Things like the boat incident are all part of the chances people took coming to China, and they cannot claim they did not know there was a war on.

The general tenor of these observations was underscored a day or so later when Bill Watson told me things had become increasingly worse. Bandits were now so prevalent on all the rivers leading to Canton that shipping was almost at a standstill. Pirates had even held up a ferry in the Canton harbor at six in the evening, then took it upstream a way where they robbed the passengers, including two foreign doctors, of money and watches. Stanvac could not move any stock to up-country agents or outlets. The company did not own boats that could carry goods past Canton, and Chinese shipping lines were not leaving Canton at that time. Bill added that our agents were beginning to show the first signs of fear, and he thought that a major crisis for the government was not very far away. This would be hastened if one of the British river boats were blown up, as the pirates had threatened to do.

People were also beginning to wonder if bandits would attack Shameen as well. The island was quite open and vulnerable, and an attack would not be difficult to carry out. Police protection of a sort was on hand, but from superficial observation the police spent most of their time sleeping or playing marbles with the children on Shameen. Pete found two of them playing on his daughter's swing one evening, probably a good indicator of the level of police alertness and responsibility.

Despite these ominous developments, Bill Watson called me into his office toward the end of the first week in December to say he wanted me to make an inspection trip to Kongmoon, a town almost directly south from Canton but not too far away. Travel would be by Chinese river boat, in the company of another employee from the Canton office. The objective was to see the place, meet and talk to the local agents, and learn whatever possible about conditions in the area. Following this trip I was to become responsible for supplying this part of the Canton territory.

The following Tuesday my colleague and I set out for Kongmoon by tow boat. These boats, I wrote, "...are about 100 feet long, 35 feet wide, and carry about 300 passengers. They have two big rooms on each of two decks, the walls of which are lined with double decker beds. These are actually one big double decker bed on which passengers are separated from each other only by wooden slats. Men and women are assigned indiscriminately. Passengers either stand or sit on the portion of the big double bed assigned them; no general sitting area was available. The space in the middle of the room is left empty, and is the site of constant entertainment and the hawking of traditional medicines and other consumer goods; music blares almost continually.

"The furnishings are perhaps best described as the Chinese version of what a well-appointed room should be. There are many brass fittings gleaming in the lamp light, mirrors filled with gold characters, a huge eye that surveys the whole room, and a large photograph of some man at one end, in a sort of shrine-like arrangement, complete with flowers. This was probably a recently deceased owner of the boat, or some close relative of the owner. The entrance to the vessel is amidship, a small hall separates the two sleeping rooms, and that's it. The coolie class downstairs is the same, only no brass fittings, and I suspect they sweep the floor less often."

A China Story: From Peip'ing to Beijing

Although these boats are little more than barges, and are pulled by launches, they make pretty fair speed, especially when the current is with them. Because of the piracy threat, the boats travelled in packs of four or more, accompanied by a gun boat. The wood-burning tugs sent up showers of sparks that looked like giant Roman candles in the darkness. Ahead one could see the lights from the accompanying boats as they moved down the river; overhead were millions of stars. The shore was completely dark; not a light showed for miles, but on the tops of the hills one could see the outlines of pagodas.

We arrived in Kongmoon fairly early the following morning, met at the landing by an impressive delegation of agents and their associates. I remember being taken off for a welcoming coffee consisting of a half cup of coffee, mixed with a half cup of sweetened condensed milk, and a raw egg thrown in. This was actually pretty tasty. The inspection visit proved instructive in many ways, but the schedule was crammed very full and was very tiring, not helped by my having a nasty cold and the weather being very wet and dreary.

The agents were indeed becoming anxious, over both the banditry that was so prevalent in their own back yard and the news of continuing deterioration of the Nationalist position in the far north. Being men of substance in their community, they had good reason to be fearful that the Communists might prevail. They doubted the Nationalists could hold the Communists off in the long run, however, because they believed the Nationalists lacked the capacity to carry through the reforms required to be successful. Although I thought the meetings had gone well on the whole, there was much to feel frustrated about, and some of the glamour had certainly worn thin. Perhaps most of all, I became intensely aware that the course of events coming up in China would pose cruel dilemmas for the people about to be caught up in them.

Seated on my bunk in the river boat on the trip home, surrounded by my fellow passengers, each sitting in his or her allotted bunk space, I wrote my impressions to Lyn in pretty gloomy terms: "[The trip left me] surfeited with dreary, dim rooms, dirty streets, hard beds, Chinese shouting in my ear, politeness and filth, being stared at, being tired, filled with tea, shark's fin soup and abalone, dealing with evasiveness and being misunderstood purposely or innocently, and cold and crowded boats. Having now seen a little of China behind the big cities and foreign sections, I feel very sorry for the Chinese who live in it. This really isn't meant to be whining, but I wanted a taste of China and I suppose I took too big a bite the first time...with a Chinese opera blasting out of the radio in the big sleeping room of the boat, and trying to write under the stares of my neighbors, the fun part of the trip was not very much in evidence." I had finally realized that China appeared more romantic and serene when viewed from the deck of a luxury river boat than it did on the ground, but it was inevitable that I would learn that lesson at some point.

My view of things mellowed considerably once back in Canton, bathed, fed, and warmed by the fireplaces in the apartment. The event that now took all my attention was the expected arrival of Lyn on December 21st, only a few days after my own return. While content with the steady letter writing that kept us in close touch, the sudden awareness that Lyn would arrive in a matter of days made me anxious and suddenly impatient. This must have showed, for the Petersons asked if I hoped the week would pass quickly. I had not talked about Lyn's visit very widely, and was trying to be calm about it, so the question surprised me. When I answered with a "yes," the Petersons smiled sort of knowingly and passed on to something else.

CHAPTER EIGHT

MUKDEN PLACED UNDER CENSORSHIP; MANY STARVE IN COMMUNISTS' SIEGE

New York Times, December 27, 1947, p.1

CANTON MOB FIRES BRITISH CONSULATE; SIX BRITONS INJURED, AMERICANS GET THREATS AS CHINESE PROTEST KOWLOON AFFAIR

New York Times, January 17,1948, p. 8

Canton/Hongkong, Christmas/New Year, 1947/48

The waiting finally ended; Lyn arrived as scheduled. The reunion was a happy, emotional one, accompanied by stomach butterflies of anticipation and sudden shyness on both our parts. But this was soon over, and it was as though we had never separated. The Watsons insisted Lyn stay with them instead of with a Shell secretary, which was most generous and thoughtful. They gave us maximum freedom to come and go as we pleased, and imposed a minimum of social obligations. The time was the Christmas season, though, and parties were being given everywhere. In the process Lyn met the oil company people, State Department people, my bachelor sports/gambling/drinking cronies and the young unmarried set, such as it was. My letters to Lyn had described many of these people, but even so she had to absorb a large number of names and faces in a short time.

I believe the only Chinese Lyn met was Ah T'ung, the cook/houseboy Ron and I had never made much effort to understand or to educate. Although we complained to each other, and outsiders, about his cooking and other housekeeping shortcomings, we rarely bothered to bring our concerns to his attention or encourage him to improve his ways in any respect. Lyn changed all that. She expressed pleasure at meeting him, complimented him on the way he kept the apartment, praised his cooking and asked him about his specialties, and generally treated him as a human being. Ah T'ung blossomed under this unexpected civility and personal interest. He smiled, he became talkative, he rushed around making certain that things were picked up and clean, and the food actually became quite tasty. He also made discreet soundings as to whether Lyn would be coming to stay permanently in the apartment, and was obviously disappointed to learn that this was not likely to happen soon, if ever.

With Ron's active participation, we set about decorating the apartment for Christmas. A tree went up in the living room, complete with a little Santa Claus at the top. For trimmings there were colored globes with little fish in them, little man figures suspended by strings attached to their caps, paper chains that Lyn and Ron put together, and a string of erratically functioning lights; a wreath was hung on the door. Lyn made an attractive fruit arrangement in a bowl on the dining table, and put flowers in a Mongolian hat stand we had picked up somewhere. With a fire in the fireplace, candles lighted on the mantle, and the tree lights blinking, the living room actually became a festive and happy place. Our quarters had suddenly become livable and pleasant, a model of what the apartment could be if someone bothered to take the time and effort to spruce it up.

We had Christmas Eve dinner with the Watsons who, ever the gracious host and hostess, produced a lovely holiday spread. Lyn and "E" took to each other immediately; they found much that was similar in their outlooks and the way they reacted to situations, and they chatted away as though they had been friends for years. Dinner was a thoroughly pleasant experience, with good food and good conversation, but I was anxious to get away nevertheless. As soon as seemed reasonable to do so, we excused ourselves on grounds that a walk would help settle the large meal we had just completed.

By the time we left the Watsons' apartment it was evening and quite dark, chilly but not actually cold. We walked along the bund, past the apartment, and into the yard of the little Anglican church where the Malcolms had married. There were lights in the lamps of houses lining the walkways, and lights glowed in the sampans moored at the bund, all of which threw interesting shapes and shadows on the face of the church through the branches of trees. We stepped inside the wall that surrounded the churchyard, and I brought out my Christmas present for Lyn — an engagement ring, purchased a week or so earlier in a jewelry shop in the city. I held the ring out with a mixture of hope and anxiety, for I was not totally certain of the response.

I need not have worried; then and there we agreed that a life together was something we both wanted. In our letters we had talked through, so to speak, the risks and pitfalls marriage could entail. The outcome was not exactly a surprise, therefore, but in the offering and accepting of a ring any doubts we had about each other at the end of summer were finally dispelled. We would now be engaged, formally, officially, and openly, but before that Lyn had a couple of conditions that had to be resolved.

The first of these was Lyn wanted to keep her maiden name. She could not explain why she wanted to do this, only that it was important to her. The second condition was more operational. Lyn did not want to ever discuss (read argue) money matters in a marriage. Her father and mother had fought over money as long as she could remember, and she did not want to repeat that experience. Lyn felt her father berated her mother unfairly for spending recklessly on everything, while her mother struggled to make ends meet on budgets that were imposed on her and always inadequate. Lyn reasoned that any money we had would be for us to spend and save as a family, that she would surely spend money only in the interest of the family as a whole, and if I could not trust her to do that I should not be asking to marry her.

We talked about this for a while, and after a bit I made a counter proposal: if Lyn would take my name in marriage, I would promise never to argue about money matters or question any money decision she might make, although we would certainly talk over major money decisions together. This was easy for me to accept because Lyn's position on money was basically a very sensible one. There was another pause while Lyn gave my response some thought, and then we had an agreement. The engagement was now truly "on."

The evening had become too chilly to linger very long in the churchyard, although admittedly there was a glow to the moment that partly compensated for the night air. Arm in arm we returned to the Watsons' and told them what had just happened. They were warm in their congratulations and pleased with our

85

news, and we all began immediately to discuss strategies to bring about a change in the Stanvac marriage policy.

Bill Watson argued that I should write a letter to Stanvac, one that was clear and concise, stating that I had become engaged. The letter would describe Lyn's background, and further state we planned to marry at the end of the school year when Lyn's contract with PAS would be at an end. I was unwilling to be placed in the position of asking a corporation for permission to marry, but Bill argued this would only be reporting a change in my bachelor status. Whatever came of this, he felt it only fair to raise the issue with the company. Any decision after an answer came back would be up to us, but it was important, at least, to write. No decisions would be made on these matters that night, of course, but from that point on the Watsons became active partisans on our side in the showdown that would be played out over the coming two months.

The following night, Christmas, we announced our engagement to a group gathered in the apartment. This was a happy and raucous occasion, and at one point we all signed a handkerchief on which the facts about the engagement had been written. I do not know what became of the handkerchief, but I still retain a paper crown, of the kind the British wear at Christmas gatherings, which bears the words "Xmas Souvenir of Lyn's Big Error — Poor Gal," and also signed by everyone. Now all knew we were engaged, and it was a relief to have this a secret no more.

The rest of the holiday week passed in a happy blur, and all too fast. I had to be at work on the regular working days, but "E" took Lyn with her on the usual rounds, including trips into the city. On one occasion Lyn accompanied me to inspect gasoline stations, and in the course of doing that we came across a large and colorful funeral procession passing along a main street. As we watched and waited for it to pass, the lead band took a turn and marched off into a side street, the coffin and mourners continued on straight ahead. A second band, bringing up the rear, took a turn into yet another side street, but in an opposite direction from the first. We never knew if this dispersion was part of the funeral program or, if not, whether they all came together again somehow, but it was a puzzling sight.

In the evenings there were parties, dinners together in the apartment, or just casual socializing with people who dropped in or invited us to visit them. The Watsons told us soon after Lyn's arrival that a new batch of visitors was coming to stay with them for New Year's, and suggested that Lyn and I go to Hong Kong to spend New Year's Eve. That way Lyn could fly back directly to Peip'ing from Hong Kong, avoiding a stopover in Shanghai, and give us a chance to sample the attractions of Hong Kong together.

We jumped at the chance, and with Bill's blessing and grant of the leave time needed to make the trip, the arrangements were soon made. An overnight trip on the river boat S.S. Fat Shan (the night schedule had been reinstated) brought us to Kowloon and the Peninsula Hotel on the morning of New Year's Eve. The hotel provided dormitory-like arrangements for single people at the time, four to six people of the same sex to a room, and Lyn and I checked into these accommodations. We had been looking forward to having the day and evening to ourselves, getting away from people at last after a week in the festive, if somewhat confining, atmosphere of Shameen.

When we checked in, however, I was dismayed to find a note waiting for me from George Behrman, deputy manager of the Stanvac office in Hong Kong, and someone I did not know well at all. The note invited Lyn and me to spend New Year's Eve with him at his home on Victoria Island, the commercial and governmental center of the Crown Colony across the harbor from Kowloon. A car and driver would be waiting for us at the Star Ferry terminal on Victoria, and Mr. Behrman was looking forward to meeting us and getting to know us better. This was an invitation we could not refuse, much as I wanted to do so, and I thought I saw the fine hand of Bill Watson behind it all. How else could Mr. Behrman know we would be in Hong Kong, and at the Peninsula, if the Watsons had not tipped him off?

Feeling a bit cheated out of a last evening together and on the town, we dressed for dinner and set out for Mr. Behrman's. "The Peak," where Mr. Behrman lived, was (and still is) a residential area at the top of a large hill/ small mountain that overlooks the harbor below. The spacious homes located there were the residences of the cream of Hong Kong's business, governmental and professional leaders. The Behrman home was one of these, with a spectacular view heightened at night by the lights of the city and the ships at anchor.

The driver deposited us at the front gate, which a servant opened for us and then ushered us into the house, and there we were greeted by Mr. Behrman. He was very cordial and welcoming, and apologized for the fact that Mrs. Behrman would not be present as well, but unfortunately she was back in the States for some reason. We were to be the only guests that evening, he said, and I inwardly groaned at the prospect of spending New Year's Eve in the company of this "old man," who must have been all of 45 at the time. But we trooped into the living room for pre-dinner drinks, where a cheery fire was burning on the hearth, and began the process of getting acquainted.

Mr. Behrman turned out to be a man of considerable charm. He had been with Stanvac pre-war in Japan, took great interest in world affairs and the arts, and the conversation flowed easily and pleasantly. He had heard of our engagement, congratulated us on it and wished us well, but did not commit himself on whether the company might agree to let us marry before my first overseas assignment was completed. Clearly, George Behrman was in the Watson mold as a Stanvac manager; intelligent, well-read, and international in outlook, not one of the 30-year company drones. The house was beautifully furnished, and the dinner that finally arrived was excellent.

When finished with dessert, Mr. Behrman shepherded us back into the living room and announced he had to leave for a party. We were free to stay in his living room as long as we wanted, there were drinks and ice in a small bar to one side, and the servant would be available if we wanted anything else. Finally, he had ordered a car to be available to take us back to the harbor anytime after midnight we were ready. With that he turned down the lights, switched on the radio to a station playing quiet music, and wished us a very Happy New Year and safe journeys back to our respective destinations.

The evening could not have been better. There we were, by ourselves after all, in a lovely living room before a glowing fire, music in the background, and someone on hand to provide anything we might want. We spent the evening as we were intended to, savoring the last bit of time together before the separation that would start the next day. When the New Year arrived we toasted it in, aware that the coming year would be one of the most eventful of our lives, even though we could not know how it would actually unfold. And then it was time to leave. Mentally thanking the absent Mr. Behrman profusely for his hospitality, thoughtfulness and tact, we got into the waiting car and drove down to the harbor.

The Star Ferry between Victoria and Kowloon stopped running at midnight, but there were still many small launches along the waterfront waiting to take late revelers across the harbor. We got into one that was about to leave, with several British army officers already aboard. They had been celebrating the New Year's arrival in standard military alcoholic fashion, and were already in a pretty rowdy state. We kept to ourselves on one side of the launch, leaving them to their own jostling games and comic insults, but half-way across the harbor one of them said or did something sufficiently irritating to his buddies that they picked him up bodily and tossed him into the water. This was greeted with hoots of laughter from the others, but I was concerned that the man overboard was too drunk to swim in the cold and murky water. The Chinese who was running the launch quickly turned it about, though, and sidled up to the man in the water. The boatman was probably used to this sort of playfulness from clients late in the evening. In any case, the man overboard was soon pulled into the launch and we continued our way with much guffawing and raucous comment from our fellow passengers, and a return flow of invective from the soaked and thoroughly chilled swimmer.

After landing on the Kowloon side, we started up the main street leading to the hotel, but were almost immediately accosted by another drunk, this time a merchant seaman. This one refused to let us pass until he was certain we were not Egyptians because, for some reason, he hated all Egyptians and swore to kill any he found. I tried to convince him we were Americans, not Egyptians, but he kept repeating his hatred of Egyptians over and over like a broken record. Finally, a companion who had been standing to one side while all this going on stepped forward and took the seaman by the arm, leading him away and allowing us to continue to the hotel.

Once in the hotel, we found the elevators blocked by yet another drunk, this one an American sailor in uniform. He wanted to go up to some room, but the management would not let him do so. When the sailor placed himself in an elevator car that was ready to go up, the only operator on duty would move to an adjacent car rather than carry the sailor. The sailor may have been drunk, but he was quick enough to cross over and get aboard before the operator could close the doors on the other car. This little game, back and forth between the elevators, went on for some time as we stood and watched, unable to go up ourselves while the elevators were at a standstill. The Shore Police, summoned by the management, finally arrived and took the sailor away, and with them went our last hurdle of the night.

The next morning we were driven to Kai Tak Airport, where Lyn boarded a plane for Peip'ing. The vacation had gone by all too quickly, and we were once again facing the unhappy prospect of a lengthy separation. Becoming engaged made things much happier, of course, and the outlook was considerably brighter than when we had last parted in September. But finally it was time to say good-bye, and Lyn boarded the bus that took passengers out to the plane. I watched sadly from the terminal building as passengers climbed into the waiting plane, and stayed to see the plane taxi away for takeoff. Kai Tak Airport was a daunting place in those days because the takeoff was directly into the face of a mountain that loomed at the end of the runway. I do not know how many, or indeed if any, planes failed to make it, but had heard pilots did not like the field. Somehow, it always seemed the last possible minute before a plane could gain enough altitude to make the turn and fly around the mountain.

I watched until sure that Lyn's plane would make it safely into the air, then turned and headed for the train station. The trip back to Canton by train was less pleasant and less scenic than by boat, but it was a little faster. The coaches were old, the seats wooden, the windows open, and little platforms at each end of the car reminded me of the freight car cabooses one saw on trains at home. By evening I was back on Shameen and the whole grand Christmas visit was over.

Canton, January 1948

Office work had piled up over the holidays, and there were several deadlines pressing me. A report on the Kongmoon inspection trip was due, as was a report on the service station rehabilitation program for Canton. The work was, in some ways, welcome because its urgency meant there was no time to daydream and think about Lyn and events of the past week or so.

The community's response to Lyn's visit, however, was enthusiastic and wide-spread. According to Ron, all Shameen thought Lyn was wonderful and everyone was much impressed; they also thought me a very lucky man. All during that first week people went out of their way to say how much they had enjoyed meeting Lyn, what a nice person she seemed, and how pleased they were at our engage-ment. These comments seemed genuine because they sounded spontaneous and enthusiastic, more so than mere politeness usually generates, and I felt a very fortunate young man.

After a week the reports were finally finished, and the time had come to write "the letter," as it was coming to be identified in my mind. Reaching this stage of clearing the decks, so to speak, my outlook brightened considerably, and was reflected by my whistling one day in the office. One of the Chinese staff, who had been studying very hard to improve his English, asked: "What is the happy occasion of your great rejoicing, Mr. Hendry?" One could only imagine what this man's English teacher must be like, because the previous day this student had commented to Ron: "The vision of a man hard at his work is inspiringly reminiscent of the flight of an eagle with wings wide spread." This all reminded me of a favorite phrase gleaned from one of the Chinese lesson books we had used in Peip'ing: "It is not that the mountain is high, it is only that the airplane is flying low." So much for helpful (silly?) phrases to help one learn another language; however stilted the man's English may have been, he played a terrific game of ping pong.

A couple of drafts of "the letter" finally appeared, then discussed, analyzed and pulled apart by both Watsons, and one of them was a version both approved. Addressed to Bill Watson, the letter gave something of Lyn's background and work in Peip'ing, and concluded with a final paragraph:

"Because we are both 26 years of age, we feel that a wait of two years or more would make us older than we wish to be when starting married life. Before leaving Peip'ing for my first assignment here in Canton, we had decided we would be married as soon as possible, and were unofficially engaged. It was not until the past Christmas holidays, when my fiancée came to Canton, that the announcement was made. She has returned to Peip'ing and it is our wish to be married in June when the present school term is completed. Her leave of absence expires at that time, and she must inform the school authorities in San Francisco of her intention either to return home and resume her regular teaching assignment or remain in China as my wife. In view of this, I am writing to request a ruling in this case in order that my fiancée and I may make our decisions regarding the future." In this final form the letter did not actually ask Stanvac for permission to get married, but informed the company of the options we were considering and asked for some reaction.

Bill Watson sent the letter on to the general manager in Shanghai with an official covering letter from himself, short and to the point, recommending approval for getting married and giving us his blessings. He also sent a personal note to the general manager stressing that Lyn had been a childhood friend of one Harry Strick in Palo Alto, and they played in the same string quartet there. Harry Strick, who was at that time working for Stanvac somewhere else in Asia, had also been a contemporary of mine in the same language school company at Yale during the war. Somehow, he had been permitted to marry on his first tour abroad. Bill's note stressed that the same privilege should be given me, intimating that if this were not done people in Palo Alto would be shocked to learn of such a wide discrepancy in "Company Policy." Bill seemed to think this was a powerful set of circumstances in our favor, and plugged it for all it was worth. Though skeptical that "people" in Palo Alto, whoever they might be, would care much one way or another about Stanvac's policy inconsistencies, I did not argue the point.

Having committed ourselves to getting married by June, at the latest, it was time to come to grips with the financial realities of such a move. I wrote to Lyn: "Figuring June as the date... we'll have about $1500 in the checking account, $160 in the savings account, and $500 in war bonds...This doesn't leave much room for the so-called finer things of life, but it should last until something comes along to replenish it. We'll have clothes on our back, varying amounts of fat to live on, and each other." Considering the alternative of staying with Stanvac, we might not be much better off after two more years. The young marrieds I knew in the company all complained that even with larger living allowances and higher salaries they were losing money and not building up any savings.

Much thought had also been given to job prospects when/if we went back to the U.S., but everything seemed to have a drawback. Either the nature of the work made each possibility unattractive, or the skills and training required to enter it were daunting. There came a point where I wrote: "The experience I'm getting here is of highly doubtful value as a means of working into anything except another job just like it...Even though I feel staying with Stanvac I would come out much better than most of the others, [the job] falls short of what I want ...by being a job that I really have little interest in seeing done....Right now I can stand it...but in time I'd either be absorbed by it, or I'd hate it. That's why you'll never hear me complain you took me away from Stanvac in China."

A China Story: From Peip'ing to Beijing

A letter from Bill Wells, then stationed in Hankow, reported he had heard of our engagement, but wanted more details so he would know how much to say, if asked. He added that if I were to leave Stanvac and get married, this would be the first in what would prove to be a rather large exodus. Bill had met someone in Nanking, and was transferred to Hankow for the same reason I was assigned to Canton, i.e., to cool down a potentially serious romantic interest. Undoubtedly, Bill was including himself in the projection of those who might leave the company, though his letter did not go that far. As it turned out, whatever Lyn and I decided to do, I would not be the first to leave. Nate Zimmerman told me he had decided to resign from Stanvac in February and return to the U.S. to marry his fiancée.

The social scene on Shameen continued pretty much as usual. The Petersons' second child was, by early January, more than one month late. Edna was climbing lots of stairs, but people had begun to lose interest in the event. One of my bachelor friends, an International Telephone and Telegraph (ITT) classman named Perkins, was diagnosed as having a mild case of diabetes, but tended to shrug it off as a comfortable kind of disease to have; baseball playing was put on hold because the weather had turned wet and chilly; I continued to play tennis now and then with Lou Nordeen, a Caltex classman, but on several occasions we wore gloves because it was so cold.

One evening at the Watsons' there was a spirited discussion over a proposal to sponsor a tea party. The stimulus for the idea came from a member of the consulate staff, who thought it would be nice if the American Association of South China gave a tea party for the second-ranking member of the U.S. Embassy in Nanking, due to visit Canton in the near future. Bill Watson had been the treasurer of the Association the previous year, but a new treasurer had not yet taken charge of the funds. When the consulate person asked Bill to hand over some funds, Bill refused saying that the funds had been collected for charitable purposes. In his opinion, the proposed tea party for the Embassy visitor did not fall into the category of "charity" by any stretch of imagination, so Bill would hang onto the money.

The consulate man, obviously miffed at this response, then observed that all members of the American community on Shameen should be asked to donate a little something, and proceeded to suggest that the missionary people in the outlying districts should be urged to provide food and money for the occasion as well. "E" bridled at this, calling it a dirty trick to make missionary people pay their way to the one affair on Shameen they might ever be invited to attend. She also refused to head a committee of Shameen American women for the occasion because she felt the tea party should be strictly a State Department affair, and the local State Department people should run it. "E" did not mind donating some food, but if the consulate people thought entertaining this visitor was so important they should foot most of the bill themselves. In fact, she added, they were not so slow in throwing parties at other times, and it was not clear why they were being so picky about this particular visit.

The Watsons' stand seemed very reasonable to me, and I admired the feistiness with which they held their ground. I was only peripherally involved in the whole issue, and did not even know there was an American Association of South China, let alone what the group was all about. The incident did illustrate, though, why people, after three years of facing petty problems like this in some small post overseas, are more than ready for home leave.

Canton, January 16, 1948

For some time after the war, Chinese had been streaming into the Crown Colony of Hong Kong hoping to find work and recoup from the damage and turmoil that was post-war China. Lacking means and contacts, for the most part, these refugees simply moved into vacant areas of Kowloon where they built crude huts and lived a hand-to-mouth existence. Sanitary conditions in these squatters' settlements were grim, and the crowded conditions posed all kinds of problems in terms of maintaining order and preventing disease outbreaks from spilling into the rest of the Colony. Moreover, as time passed more and more illegal immigrants swarmed into these settlements, adding constantly to the seriousness of the problem. Finally, at the start of the new year, British authorities acted by forcibly evicting squatters from their hovels and razing their settlements to the ground.

Reaction within China was immediate, angry and vociferous. The Chinese press featured the incident prominently, and a variety of groups such as students, labor unions, and patriotic societies held demonstrations protesting the British harsh treatment of the poor and homeless Chinese squatters in Kowloon. This all occurred at a time when the Nationalist government was slowly, but clearly, ceding ground to the Communists in different parts of Manchuria and north China. The plight of the Kowloon squatters provided a chance to divert public attention to a new problem, one where Chinese could give vent to nationalist feelings and nationalist pride without any likelihood the British would retaliate for insults received or threats implied.

Anti-British feelings were running high in Nanking and Shanghai, and in Canton the police notified foreign establishments to keep their foreign staff off the streets as a precaution. By noon of January 16th, a crowd of about 2,000 had assembled on Shameen and began demonstrating in front of the British Consulate. At one point, someone in the crowd tore down the British flag, and soon after the mob poured into the building, looting first and then starting to burn what they could not cart away.

At the end of the day I wrote to Lyn, putting down images of what I had seen and summarizing by saying "... flames are eating up what is left of some of the finest buildings on Shameen, and you can hear every now and then the crash as a wall or roof crumbles. I have just seen an ugly sight...a mob looting, burning, destroying, injuring ...The British Consulate is completely destroyed, so is the Chartered Bank, Jardine's Shipping Company, and the Butterfield and Swire Shipping Company. The Hong Kong Shanghai Bank, where the Stanvac office was located, was ransacked but not burned. The British gardens are tangled and uprooted, the flag pole is bent in half and the possessions of people who lived in the houses are either totally lost or some few remain scattered over the lawns and walks. The mob has dispersed, and soldiers and police have finally restored order, but a quarter of Shameen is gone."

There was a balcony outside the Stanvac office on the second floor of the Hong Kong Shanghai Bank building. Several of us stood there and watched as the riot moved down the central promenade of Shameen. "From the balcony we saw them go into Jardine's — first went the windows, then inside they went and soon smoke and flames were billowing out and people were jumping from the second story windows. Clothing, furniture, children's toys, anything, was thrown out and burned in a special bonfire on the ground in front of the building. By this time the whole central section of Shameen was ablaze — the mobs had been at it for three hours, and still no effort was made to stop them or control the flames. The mob finally started for our office, and as we went out the back they were going through the windows of the bank downstairs. Before much damage could be done to us the troops finally arrived, and the mob was beaten back."

Still writing about the scene from the office balcony, "The fury and inhumanity were frightening — nothing could stand up to it. As we watched we saw Curtis, an Australian... in the center of the mob, pale and shaken, protected by two policemen. The mob would hit him and spit on him, but didn't try to take him from the police. There was nothing we could do but watch — to go down ourselves would never have helped, only angered the mob more. Curtis was led to safety, but was badly battered." Later, the news came that when the mob took Curtis to the American Consulate building, an official there pronounced him an American citizen, opened the iron gate just enough to let him slip into the grounds, and kept him in the Consulate until order was restored.

All sorts of scenes witnessed that day came back as I continued, "The British people — amazingly calm and collected yet angry and superior in their justifiable anger — going out of their way to be polite and civil to any Chinese who spoke to them...The pathetic sight of intimate personal items, bunched together in piles — toothbrushes, old shoes, blankets, a can of baby powder...The absolute, utter wreckage of the consulate — bits of red and blue flag, glass, a chair, and the sight of the British emblem on the face of the building, flames and ruins forming a background, hanging awry...Mrs. Lawrence [wife of the Shell manager] smiling, and carrying a birthday cake that she was going to have for a children's party this afternoon."

Martial law was imposed by the end of the day, and "... troops guard the bridges, and periodically play fire hoses on the mob, which is still trying to storm back onto the island. All British women and children are being evacuated in the morning ...Only two people are badly hurt, several are bruised, some kicked and some stoned. It is surprising many weren't killed ... Even the fans on the ceiling of the Consulate were bent out of shape, huge stone figures smashed in the garden, rooms completely stripped, [and] the floors a sea of broken glass and bits of wood and cloth."

The failure of the army, police and fire department to act quickly and effectively was extremely worrisome. "It was fairly obvious that the main damage was done by those whose main interest was looting ... the students were in it, but I don't think they were responsible for the damage. To me, the real crime was the inaction, the non-interference by all the Chinese — the police, the officials, the army, the students who should realize what this can do to a China needing foreign aid so badly, and the average citizen. They all took the attitude that the British had it coming to them, and passed it off as one of those things that happen every now and then. The attitude is significant, I think, though the damage and waste will be classed as an 'incident' in newspaper articles and future accounts."

The riot in Canton turned out to be the most serious reaction in China to the Kowloon affair, though there were demonstrations in other cities, and in Shanghai both Americans and British were the targets of the crowd's hostility; reaction to the riot in Peip'ing, however, was mild. Over the next few days things gradually returned to normal, though the smell of charred wood and smoke hung over the island for some days, and the wreckage of buildings on all sides was a visible reminder of what had taken place.

What might come after the riot was not clear, but there was general agreement whatever it was would not be good for China. One interpretation that emerged believed the more corrupt and irresponsible elements of the ruling Kuomintang Party had secretly encouraged the rioting, in particular by doing nothing to curb it quickly. This was done to embarrass Dr. T.V. Soong, brother of Mme. Chiang Kai Shek, and a major political figure in South China. Since T.V. Soong represented a voice in the Kuomintang that seemed moderate and relatively progressive in contrast to others, the British were restrained in their response in order not to undercut him, but it was certain the government gained little advantage from the riot.

Foreigners worried that anti-foreign sentiment, always near the surface even among educated Chinese, would be encouraged by the fact the government did little to protect foreigners when violence turned against them. Memories of the Boxer Rebellion died hard, and people like Ron Carey, who had grown up in China, could remember when there had been incidents on Shameen with British marines at the bridges and gunboats on the river, and mobs trying to storm the island. Among the young foreigners on Shameen there was a decided change in outlook. Many were beginning to question whether there was any future to staying with their companies in China, but few had any real alternative in mind.

For us, the riot only reinforced our determination to marry and leave China, even if Stanvac agreed to the marriage; more and more, staying with the company in China looked hazardous, and unlikely to last for two more years anyway. The letter concerning marriage plans had been referred to the New York head office for a policy ruling, but I was rapidly losing interest in what the outcome might be.

Canton, Late January 1947

In the aftermath of the riot there was a return to patterns of life normal for that time and place. People went to work as usual, social life resumed, the British women and children returned from their forced evacuation, and the pace of life on Shameen continued with hardly a hiccup. Even the visible reminders of the outbreak were becoming muted. The rubble was cleared away, restoration work on the British Consulate began, and there was even progress in cleaning up some of the gardens. Armed guards and sandbag emplacements continued to grace the entrances to Shameen, but the traffic they supervised entering and leaving was back to the usual mixture of servants, employees and tradesmen. In time even the gutted buildings came to seem natural, as though they had always been that way, burned in some long ago and forgotten incident.

Our correspondence was increasingly focused on agonized discussion of what to do over the next few months. Al Pickering, a very senior Stanvac official rumored to become the next General Manager in China, visited Canton about this time. According to "E", Pickering told her he had met Lyn on some occasion or other, probably in Peip'ing when visiting the language students there, and had been very favorably impressed. "E" reported he hoped the company would allow us to marry because, in his words, "[Lyn] would raise significantly the average intelligence quotient of the company wives." Although I spoke with Mr. Pickering on several occasions, both in the office and at social gatherings, the subject of marriage did not come up until he was about to leave. At that point he came over to my desk and said he hoped the company would rule favorably on our case. This was gratifying to hear, because it meant that people such as

Pickering, Behrman and, of course, Bill Watson were on our side, all of them managers I had come to like and admire.

On the other hand, my own feelings about the company and any future role I might have in it had reached a stage where I did not want to continue with it, whatever the policy on marriage might become. The rationale for this decision was set forth in a lengthy letter to Lyn, partly to get my thoughts down on paper and thus organize them, but also to convince Lyn that I was not acting on some temporary whim. The first concern was interest in the job itself, based on what I could make of it from experience thus far.

"...I can't, and I've tried, work up more than an extremely casual interest in oil — its production, sale, refining, shipment, prices, and policies of the company all leave me extremely cold... I may never find the thing that will bring the most enjoyment in doing, but to stop looking for it, simply for security of a sort, seems foolish and unrealistic ... Regardless of my indecision as to what I'll do once we're home, I know this isn't what I want, and as the years pass I'd regret more and more having stayed with the company."

A second point concerned company life in China. "Though we could probably make our own life out here, and be happy...it would mean continually fighting for the right to live our own lives, searching for our happiness, and getting it by hook, crook or patchwork. Staying on would mean not owning a home until we retire, moving every few years, sending the children to the States for an education, and fighting to keep them from becoming just like the others they'd play with, spoiled and shallow, and it would mean separations." Added to this, I had become convinced staying with the company as a married couple would be costly for us, and after two years we could find ourselves less ready to strike out on our own than we already were. All of which seemed to lead to one conclusion, and that was to leave China in June at the latest, no matter how the company ruled. This would save time in the long run because finding a career I wanted to pursue could prove a lengthy process, and the sooner I started the better.

Having crossed the decision points of becoming engaged and picking the month of June as the best time to get married and leave China, we now concerned ourselves with the follow-up aspects of those decisions. I wrote to Lyn's parents expressing my wish to marry their daughter, and received a very warm and generous response that gave their approval and welcomed me into their family. Lyn's mother even expressed the hope that Lyn would make a good wife for me, an attitude that Lyn resented long before feminist views became widely accepted. Lyn's sister, Teddy, also wrote a supportive letter about our marriage plans, and mentioned the possibility she might fly out for the wedding, wherever and whenever that took place. The prospect of spending a honeymoon with Teddy tagging along was not something I relished, but it seemed churlish to object if she wanted to spend the time and money to travel to China just to attend a wedding. The location of the wedding was actually up in the air at that point, whether it should be Peip'ing, Canton or Hong Kong, but more and more the choice was tending toward one of the latter two locations. My own preference was for Hong Kong. Even though few people we knew might be present, there would be a chance to spend a few days of honeymoon at Repulse Bay, an elegant resort outside the crowded city areas.

At the same time I had also written to my family, telling them I was planning to marry Lyn and would probably leave Stanvac to do so. Their reply was pretty much what I expected. After making appropriate noises to the effect they were pleased I had found someone to marry, the bulk of their letter was filled with reasons why I should not get married and resign from the company. My father was particularly disturbed I would be failing to honor the implicit conditions of my employment. Not only would this be wrong, he felt, but could place a blot on my record that would plague me in future attempts to get a job. He clearly thought I was about to jettison my chances for the future in exchange for some immediate satisfaction. Though he did not make it explicit, I knew he meant "some woman" had clouded my thought processes, and was leading me down a dangerous and uncertain path. My step-mother, for her part, added support to my father's negative reaction by sounding themes of caution such as "most good things in life require sacrifice," and "haste makes waste."

These responses reflected their own experience. My father had a rough time in the latter years of the Depression, and was very aware that jobs could be lost and careers derailed on very short notice. He also knew from direct experience how difficult it was to find a replacement as good as a job lost. In fact, he was concerned over his own job security at the time he was writing, and thus pessimistic generally on this whole jobs issue. His second marriage had been delayed for some time because of economic uncertainties, so he was not sympathetic with my seeming impatience either.

I sent their letter to Lyn and tried to explain this background, and maybe soften their considerably less than enthusiastic acceptance of our marriage. I also added, "...my parents don't seem to realize I'll be doing the company a favor by leaving if I'm not planning to stay for 30 years. All the time I stay here, the company will be paying me and housing me, and if I leave after the first three years, instead of in June, the money would be wasted as far as Stanvac is concerned. In strict conscience, leaving soon seems the fairest thing I could do, and I think the company might feel the same way. As far as recommendations go, they'd be no better after three years, either. In fact, they might not be as good, if they give me one at all."

Although another letter went to my family, trying to address some of their concerns, in retrospect this had no effect; they always retained the view I made a fundamental error getting married when and how I did. My parents' unwillingness to accept Lyn from the very start was thus a disappointment, though an anticipated one, and foreshadowed the strained relations we were to have with them throughout their lifetimes.

By the end of the month preparations were underway everywhere to celebrate the coming Chinese New Year. I was told another trip was due shortly after that, this time to a place called Tsamkong, somewhere near the Indo-China border. No one seemed to know how one got there — only one or two company people had ever visited the place — but the trip sounded interesting despite my disenchantment with up-country travel after my Kongmoon trip.

Meanwhile, the city streets seemed more packed than usual, the stores filled with goods, and everywhere lamps, lanterns and masks were starting to appear. The scene was noisy, dirty, confusing and colorful all at once. The new year certainly would not be a happy one for the Chinese; rather, one more year to add to Chinese history, another year of hardship and misery, of inferiority and shame, and frustration for those who think about it because there seemed no answer. But the flowery signs and the red lanterns went up, debts were paid and corners swept; the old customs went on, quaint and ludicrous... and the flimsy paper imitations of articles may have been more representative of actual conditions than people realized.

CHAPTER NINE

> *"The present civil war in China is bitter and violent. In Manchuria, it is now a war of mass battles, artillery attacks, and heavy casualties. Current reports indicate that the military situation there is not only explosive, but is actually exploding, and the fate of the remaining Nationalist troops in that region is highly uncertain... Nationalist leaders in Peip'ing have their eyes fixed anxiously on the northeast, where the outcome of the fighting in Manchuria will inevitably affect Peip'ing's position."*
>
> A. Doak Barnett, <u>China on the Eve of Communist Takeover</u>. Frederick A. Praeger, 1963, p. 37. [Reporting on the situation in February 1948]

Canton, February 1948

On the morning of February 7th, Bill Watson called me into his office and showed me a letter sent to all offices in the China Division regarding the marriage of classmen. The letter contained the ruling of the Board of Directors on a Shanghai Office proposal that classmen over 26, with two year's service, be allowed to marry. The Board's ruling was there would be no change in policy because strong opposition to change had been voiced in "some quarters." The Shanghai Office letter, after quoting this decision, added that the letter could be taken as a reply to those classmen who had asked for permission to marry during their first term.

Bill Watson, while expressing great doubt this might be useful, suggested I write a letter to the Shanghai office to ask if this ruling were applicable to our case. The grounds for this request would be my letter had been forwarded to the New York office for a specific ruling, and therefore should be handled differently

103

from others. I agreed to write a letter for Bill's signature, but felt certain any answer would be negative.

In reporting this to Lyn, I wrote in terms of great relief the issue had finally been settled, looking forward to a wedding in June, and excited and alive again. The agonizing over what to do was ended; ahead lay preparation for the wedding, getting a job search under way, and deciding where to settle when we reached the States.

Two days later it was the Chinese New Year, the first one I had ever seen. Again writing to Lyn, "All night long the city has been like a battlefield — the firecrackers make a continuous roar, as though machine guns were blasting away at something, with an occasional bomb dropping now and then...the Year of the Rat has arrived. Tomorrow there are supposed to be dragons in the streets in spite of a ban on dragon dances and pleas for austerity, and there seems to be an amazing amount of celebration and seasonal joy, especially for a country that has so little to be happy about."

The next day, walking alone through the city streets, the shops were all closed, the gutters were awash with red firecracker paper, and most buildings had red paper or red streamers plastered on them. The children all wore red, too, and the sidewalk vendors were selling candles and toys, balloons, wooden swords, flower lanterns, pictures, fruit, and firecrackers. I expected a firecracker in the face at almost every step because the practice was to stick lighted firecrackers in the gates of shops at about shoulder level, or just to throw them randomly into the air.

Despite the relief felt when Stanvac's Board finally made its decision, we discovered making choices and deciding what to do next was not going to be all that simple. For one thing, there was the distance separating us; letters took anywhere from four to ten days to move between Canton and Peip'ing. Thus, as much as three weeks might pass for questions raised in one letter to get a response in another, by which time some element in the situation might have changed. Fortunately, most letter exchanges did not take that long.

More importantly, although the basic problem was pretty straightforward, we found good reasons to keep our plans to ourselves for a while. I had reached a firm conclusion that a career with Stanvac was not what I wanted out of life. Lyn's contract with PAS called for her to stay until June, and she wanted to complete it. If I could stay in Canton with Stanvac until June, we could marry then and return home. This would meet Lyn's obligations, add a bit more income, and possibly yield savings that would be handy when starting anew in the States. From our standpoint, a June resignation, marriage and departure was the ideal combination.

But this timetable was not going to be easy to follow. Nate Zimmerman actually submitted his resignation in mid-February and was quickly dropped from the payroll, though he had wanted to stay on a while longer. He was quite bitter about this, and wrote advising me to move very cautiously. Once the company management knew a classman planned to resign they would force him to leave immediately. Nate had also heard that Bill Watson was annoyed because he had not been able to get any commitment out of me about my plans.

Stanvac classmen all over China were in something of a dither for several reasons. For one thing, they thought Nate had been given a raw deal, but several had also hoped for a change in the company marriage policy. Bill Wells and Sam Strassburger were among these, and were disappointed when the change had not come. In another matter, the company had just announced a forty percent cut in everyone's cost-of-living allowance, and some classmen were trying to set up an organized protest over this.

Further complicating things, the Canton office had a new classman on the staff, John McCubbin, who had completed his language training in February and was reporting for his first assignment. He quickly confided in me that he expected to resign in June, not because he wanted to get married but because he, too, now knew he did not want to stay with Stanvac. McCubbin was anxious that I not resign precipitously because that would put pressure on him to reveal his plans, and he was reluctant to do so.

Finally, another classman had just resigned to join the State Department. He had accepted a Stanvac job, gone through the language training in Peip'ing after applying for a foreign service appointment, and did all this knowing he would probably leave the company in a few months' time. The company managers were reportedly furious over this particular resignation, and indeed the whole marriage/resignation issue had become something of a hot issue in company circles; everyone was feeling some of the pressure from it. On February 27th the Shanghai office sent a final "no" to any departures or exceptions from the recently re-affirmed marriage policy for classmen.

Bill Watson was, in his quiet way, increasingly anxious to learn what I was thinking, and his deputy was probing the same question in his much more heavy-handed way. I could appreciate their position; if I were not going to continue in Canton they had to get a replacement as soon as possible, and from the language class that was due to finish in April. No ultimatum, of the fish-or-cut-bait variety, was ever forthcoming from Bill, but I was restive and unhappy that I could not be open and above board with him about our plans. The result was a lot of sweating, squirming, stewing and rationalizing on my part while I avoided making any commitment.

Lyn was the one to pose the simple suggestion that broke the stalemate. Why not, she asked, just resign now, come to Peip'ing and get married? We could find a place to stay until school was over, and then return to the States together. This posed obvious disadvantages for us, discussed at great length in correspondence, but I was getting so tired of dissembling that the prospect of a clean break with the company, and getting on with our own lives, was highly attractive.

So, on a Sunday morning in early March, I called on the Watsons in their apartment and told them of our decision. They were not surprised, of course, offered congratulations and best wishes to us both, and expressed regrets I was leaving Canton. Bill asked if the company's marriage policy was the reason for my decision, and I explained that it was not. He suggested that I not write a letter of resignation, but simply resign in person on my way through Shanghai. This would make it possible, he said, to explore at the same time whether the company would pay my way home, and if so under what conditions. Having my return fare paid was an unexpected possibility, but it certainly seemed worth a try and I was grateful for the advice. By resigning in person, it also meant Bill was not cutting me off the payroll immediately, but leaving the actual date for the Shanghai office to decide once they had my verbal resignation.

Having crossed this hurdle, once again there was a feeling of great relief. From now on all our plans would be in the open, and I could talk about them with anyone who would listen. We picked March 24th as the date to leave Canton, assuming reservations could be obtained on a flight to Shanghai, and flying to Peip'ing from there as soon thereafter as possible. The wedding would be held on a Saturday, April 3rd, giving us a few days to make last minute arrangements of all kinds. These included some important matters, however, one being to find a place for us to live.

The letters to Lyn now expressed eagerness to be with her again, and impatience with how slowly the next few weeks would pass. They also contained some second thoughts about leaving China: "In many, many ways I'll be glad to leave China — it's depressing, dirty, hopeless — and leaving it will be no strain at all. Yet there is, too, a great sentiment that I feel toward China — this is where we met, there is so much color and noise, so completely different from everything at home, so sad to see such a magnificent culture being torn apart by civil war, and there is definitely a feeling I have not made the best use of my time here, my own fault entirely."

We quickly agreed the wedding would be in the Peking Union Church, with Ernest Shaw as the officiating clergyman. About a hundred people would be invited to the wedding, and forty or so of these would also be invited to a reception at the Fang Chia Yuan compound. I asked Sam Strassburger to be my best man, and he readily agreed. Sam had asked me some time previously to stand with him when he married, and Lyn and I both liked Sam very much for the amiable, honest, responsible person he was. The other three classmen we trained with would be ushers, plus Don Mead who had been at language school with the rest of us. On Lyn's side, Dorie Eldred would be the Maid of Honor.

This was also a time to start the search for a new job, not easy because I had so little idea where best to look. This was a recurring theme in conversations with other classmen. After one such evening a letter to Lyn noted: "It's amazing that so many people, including, naturally, myself, who have had a pretty decent education, considerable travel, normal home life and so on, should reach their late twenties with almost no idea of how they'd like to spend their lives, or what they'd really like to do...Maybe we all expect too much, maybe we're looking for something that doesn't exist, but I really can't believe that"

So, in this muddled state of mind letters went everywhere — to Yale, to the Veterans Administration, to the Harvard Business School, follow-ups on some export-import leads Sam had given me, and the local Naval Attaché contacted some people he knew with Japan interests. My ITT colleague in Canton, Perkins, was pushing my candidacy for a job with ITT in Japan, and Bruce Tingle, a pilot with CAT, told me of a job as office manager for CAT in Shanghai that might be opening up soon. One of the Consulate General staff in Canton was thinking of leaving the foreign service and buying a small newspaper somewhere in upstate New York, and we talked over the possibilities of linking forces in some kind of joint venture. Finally, I heard from Lyn that Ernest Shaw had talked with Jim Hunter, director of the China Relief Mission (CRM) in Peip'ing, about a job with that agency after we married. This flurry of activity of course yielded nothing tangible in the short time until leaving for Peip'ing, but it did produce a cable asking me to contact the CRM headquarters in Shanghai when passing through, and I also made arrangements to visit the CAT office there.

Winding up the rest of my affairs did not take long, consisting mainly of closing my bank account, cleaning up what office work I could and handing the rest over to McCubbin, and trying to sell my radio/phonograph. There was extensive discussion with "E" Watson and Edna Peterson whether a gray pin stripe suit was suitable for a wedding, or whether I needed a new dark one. They finally agreed that I could stick with what I had, which was welcome news for the pocketbook. Ron Carey suggested sending my trunk back with the Suters, who were due to depart on home leave about the same time. This would be a considerable savings and, once the Suters agreed, all I need take to Peip'ing was clothing and personal effects, some towels, and some long white candles for the wedding, if any could be found. The shipment with the Suters never reached me back in the States, however, unhappily so because all the letters Lyn had written from Peip'ing were in it.

As the end of March approached, and after weeks of cloudy days, the Spring rains finally came, and with them the damp, humid, hot season that covers everything with mildew, warps the furniture, and drains the vitality from everyone. I was glad not be around to cope with all this.

Finally, everything was ready for me to leave Canton, and on the Saturday before my departure the Petersons invited Ron Carey and me to their apartment for a cold roast beef supper. Come up about eight, they said, and since this sort of casual invitation had come from the Petersons so many times before I thought nothing much about it. I played ball in the afternoon, took a leisurely bath, and while waiting for the time to pass Pete stopped by just before eight, presumably on his way home from some cocktail party. We had a drink, killing time until his wife would have finished nursing their new baby, and then went upstairs together.

As we walked into the living room, an assembled mob started to sing the Wedding March, and as I dazedly looked around the room I realized that all the Stanvac company people, some of the Shell people, the resident Caltex classman, some State Department people, and a scattering of others were all present. This was a "shower," and I may be one of the few men ever to be on the receiving end of one. There were toasts, speeches, and presents of all kinds, some funny and some serious. The one I remember best, though, was a large box of condoms with a note attached that read: "Warning — one of these has been punctured!"

The Petersons had laid on a lavish smorgasbord, and everyone ate mightily and drank to match as the evening progressed, Bill and "E" Watson leading the way. I was understandably in something of a cloud through all this, saying good-bye and accepting everyone's best wishes and expressions of disappointment that Lyn was not present and we were not being married in Canton. The evening certainly succeeded in giving me a positive and upbeat send-off, complete with good feelings about the people I was leaving, and grateful for their friendship and support during the trying period now at an end.

The next few days were anticlimax. Arriving in Shanghai as scheduled on the 24th, the actual resignation was accomplished quickly in a civil and business-like atmosphere. There were expressions of regret I was leaving the company, and in something of a goodwill gesture the managers informed me Stanvac would pay my return fare if I left China by June. And then it was over, an outcome totally unforeseen when, almost a year to the day earlier, I originally signed on.

One of the senior people in the headquarters had taken me aside earlier in the day and urged me not to be hasty about resigning. Take Lyn back to Canton and live with her, he advised jovially, and in a few months the company will force you to get married to avoid a scandal. Although I found his suggestion both surprising and unwelcome, and implicitly an insult to Lyn, I managed to reply only that our plans were already firm and could not be changed. In fact, looking back on the incident, this man was not insulting, only ahead of his time. The alternative he suggested for us was one my children's generation would certainly find totally sensible and unobjectionable. But the times, and attitudes, were different then.

The possible opening in the CAT Shanghai office had still not materialized, but the interview with the CRM people seemed more promising, though nothing definite was agreed. With those chores completed I cabled Lyn: "Arriving Peip'ing Sunday afternoon [the 28th] via CNAC happy excited very much in love, [signed] Jim." And on the 28th, which happened to be Easter Sunday, my plane touched down at the Peip'ing airport. I disembarked to find Lyn waiting for me, and a whole new dimension to our lives about to begin.

CHAPTER TEN

> *"Demoralization and deterioration of situation portrayed in our report of March 8 have continued at an accelerated pace. There is an increased feeling of helplessness in government circles as elsewhere and a fervent searching for some means of bringing a stop to civil war and economic political uncertainties resulting from it. There is an increasing realization, shared even by the Generalissimo, that military victory over Communists is impossible and that some other solution must be reached if Communist-domination of all China is to be avoided."*
>
> Letter from Ambassador Stuart to Secretary Marshall, dated March 31, 1948, in <u>United States Relations with China</u>, p. 845.

Peip'ing, March/April 1948

Getting together again was the easy part. Suddenly, all sorts of decisions had to be made because the wedding, so long thought of in abstract terms, was scheduled to take place the next Saturday, April 3rd, less than a week away. Fortunately, this was the Spring vacation at PAS, and Lyn was free from school duties. Many wedding details were already well in hand when I arrived, but finding a place to live after the wedding remained a high priority. I was staying with the MacFadyens, who kindly offered to put me up for as long as necessary; Lyn continued to share the old compound at Fang Chia Yuan with Dorie and a new tenant, Nell McGurk. The Scott sisters had already returned to the States sometime earlier.

The landlady who owned the compound at Fang Chia Yuan had a small set of rooms she was willing to rent to us, but these required sharing cooking and other arrangements with Dorie and Nell. Such a setup seemed less than ideal for

111

a couple of newly-weds, but there was now at least a fallback position if nothing better turned up in the next few days. What we needed was a place furnished with everything (we had nothing of our own), at an affordable price, on a short lease, and with a modicum of privacy. Housing as such was not particularly tight in Peip'ing at the time, but housing that was reasonably clean, quiet and workable was hard to find. In the course of our search we looked at a few compounds where we would share space with several other Chinese families, but the noise level and the crowded conditions in these were unacceptable to us.

Finally, and I think Neil MacFadyen put us on to it, we found a small, fully furnished apartment owned by a German nurse, long a resident of Peip'ing. The apartment was part of a larger compound and shared a courtyard with another set of living quarters, then vacant but formerly used as a bachelors' mess by Stanvac classmen attending the language school. Our part of the compound was nothing grand, but it served our purposes. Located in Hsi Tsung Pu hut'ung, a long half-block from Hatamen Street, the compound was close to PAS and reasonably convenient to the Legation Quarter and Morrison Street.

Entry off the street was through a muddy yard (probably the rear entrance of the main compound) with the kitchen and servants' quarters off to one side. Inside the apartment itself was a dining room with a pair of matching chests, a small sitting room with a sofa and a couple of chairs, a tiny bedroom that opened off the sitting room and was separated from it only by a curtain, and a bathroom at the end of a hall that also led off the sitting room. The sitting room looked out on a court, where a couple of wicker chairs and a table were available to use when the weather was pleasant. The rent was inexpensive because the landlady, like others in Peip'ing, preferred to keep the place occupied if she could. There were not many other people looking for accommodations like these at the time, and given the unpromising military/political situation in North China she did not expect a large influx of potential renters anytime soon. Whatever its drawbacks, and this first home together was a far cry from anything either of us had been used to in China, this would certainly more than do until June, when we expected to leave.

Finding servants to run the household for us turned out to be fairly easy. T'ien, the cook at Fang Chia Yuan, had an unemployed cousin named Pien whom he recommended highly to be the cook, and Pien brought with him a friend named Ho to act as houseboy and man of all work.

Pien was a rotund man of about fifty, completely bald, badly pock-marked, and with a grin that prominently featured several gold front teeth. His manner was somewhat officious, and he took himself quite seriously at times, but he was a good cook and tried hard to please. Should things did not work out with Pien, we could always exercise a bit of leverage through his sponsor, T'ien, to straighten out any problem that might arise.

Once we had a place to live, and servants to run it, we turned to other details, and here there was lots of help. Our wedding would be the first such event to be held in Peip'ing's foreign community since the end of the war, and everyone was quite excited about it. The missionary ladies who had assailed Lyn's character not long before were anxious to show they were now among her staunchest support-ers. One offered to do the flower arrangements in the church, another volun-teered to play a cello piece at the wedding, and a third wanted to sing a solo. We would even have two ministers for the wedding ceremony, one being Ernest Shaw and the other Allan Easton, pastor of the Peking Union Church. Overseeing all was Beth Shaw, who took a decidedly maternal interest in the whole affair and supervised every detail to ensure that arrangements would proceed smoothly. She also offered to bake our wedding cake, using an old family recipe to do so.

As the week wore on, Sam Strassburger and the ushers began arriving, and MacFadyen helped find them places to stay. One of the chores that remained for me was to buy champagne for the reception. A Catholic monastery outside the city walls, a place called Ch'ala, actually made champagne locally, and one day Bill Wells went with me to pick up a supply. We were greeted by a jovial lay brother who was in charge of the wine cellars, and who must have enjoyed his responsi-bilities enormously, to judge from his easygoing manner and the purplish color of his nose. After a tour of the place, and a generous sampling of the monastery's selection of other wines and cordials, we took delivery of our champagne order. Ch'ala obviously was not one of the world-class champagne labels, but it tasted like champagne and cost about one U.S. dollar per bottle. Bill and I came back with enough to make certain that champagne would, indeed, flow like water at the reception.

Plans for the reception were largely in the hands of Lyn and Dorie and their cook, because it would be held in the Fang Chia Yuan compound. The list of invi-tees, limited to about forty, included mostly young people — oil company classmen, friends and colleagues of Lyn's from PAS and the Peip'ing community — and a scattering of officialdom. The decision to limit the size, and not include all those invited to the wedding, was partly an economy measure that reflected the paucity of our resources and the uncertainty of our future. But in addition to those very real concerns, we wanted the reception to be a good time for everyone, and felt this would best be realized if attendance was kept to a small group, and one fairly homogeneous in terms of age, congeniality and people we really knew. In practical terms, parents of Lyn's students (many of them missionaries) and older acquaintances were invited only to the wedding.

Nationalist China did not require foreigners to obtain a license to be married, more or less taking the position that foreign marriages were not a Chinese concern. Marriage in China was very much a family matter, a key element in the maintenance of the family and clan structure and something to be carefully arranged between families; perhaps it was not a government matter at all, even for Chinese couples. Unlike the case for British citizens, U.S. consulates abroad did not perform civil marriage ceremonies for U.S. citizens, and no official record of a marriage was kept. A consular representative would, however, witness a wedding ceremony involving U.S. citizens and issue a certificate attesting to that fact. Consulates would also amend a passport to record that a marriage had taken place. We wanted as much evidence of our marriage as possible, so arranged for someone from the Consulate General to be present as a witness at our wedding, and two ministers would be officiating. Despite all this, something of a puzzle remained whether lack of a Chinese marriage license might some day place our relationship in some kind of legal limbo.

That first week of being together again went by very quickly, but the "things to be done" list finally fell into place. School was due to open the Monday following the wedding. Mrs. Fenn offered, as her wedding present, to act as substitute for Lyn on that Monday. This extended our honeymoon from one day to two, not counting the wedding day itself, but still not enough time to go anywhere. Conditions in the countryside surrounding Peip'ing did not encourage travel. Going to a hotel in the Western Hills, for example, was considered too risky, even for a couple of nights. There was not much point in going to T'ientsin either, with the strong possibility of indefinite delay if the rail line were cut, as it was with increasing frequency. But T'ientsin was a dreary place anyway, and accommodations there were not particularly good. The honeymoon would be spent, then, at our new home in the Hsi Tsung Pu hut'ung compound — much safer, and certainly cheaper.

For one final celebration of my bachelorhood, or its imminent demise, Neil MacFadyen threw a stag party for me on Friday, the eve of the wedding. All those present were classmen from the three oil companies. Several were people I did not know, but the core group comprised the ushers and best man from the wedding. As those things go, it met the standard criteria for a bachelor party — too much to drink, plenty to eat, and an increasing level of inanity as the evening wore on. One man, a Shell classman whom I had not met before, entertained everyone by crushing beer cans against his forehead, and someone, perhaps the same man, jumped, or fell, through a glass-topped coffee table. Before these events occurred I had decided the time had come to retire early and gracefully, if I could, in order to greet the next day with a clear head and more energy than most of the others gave signs of being able to do. And that is what I did.

Peip'ing, April 3, 1948

The day of the wedding was typical of early Spring in Peip'ing, cloudy and windy, chilly but not quite cold. The church was only a short distance from the MacFadyens' home. As the appointed time approached, Sam and I walked over, hatless and without topcoats, to wait in a small anteroom that adjoined the altar area. MacFadyen had put a Stanvac car and driver at our disposal for the day, and the driver brought Lyn and Dorie to the church. I admit to feeling slightly nervous, not so much at the prospect of marriage, but more a kind of stage fright at the thought of being married in public view. When the time arrived for the ceremony to start, Sam and I entered and stood before the altar waiting for the rest of the wedding party.

We turned to watch as Lyn came down the aisle on the arm of Henry Fenn who, acting in *loco parentis*, would give her away. She was lovely in a white silk dress, no train but with white puff sleeves, and a tiara of small flowers in her hair. The bouquet she held was trembling visibly, but she made the trip down the aisle without incident. She told me later that Dorie had counseled her, while waiting for the ceremony to begin, that it was never too late to back out if Lyn had any real doubts about marrying me. The thoughts that went through her head at that last minute may have unnerved Lyn a bit, but they did not deter her. Neither did the remark, again reported later, that Lyn heard as she went down the aisle. One of the classmen guests, seated at the end of his pew, had whispered to a neighbor as she passed by something like, "Am I glad I'm not in Hendry's shoes!"

And then we were standing together, before the two ministers, arm in arm, and repeating the venerable and always moving vows, which in this case substituted "cherish" for "obey." An exchange of rings, a decorous kiss, a final prayer, and it was all over. Following the Malcolms' example at their Canton wedding, I hustled Lyn back down the aisle at a fast pace, just short of actually running, to wait outside the front door and greet the guests as they emerged from the church. I must have thought fast was a stylish way to make a wedding exit. The Malcolm wedding was one of the few I had ever attended, and was thus a model of sorts, but the haste drew a certain amount of unfavorable comment afterward.

One of the guests never actually got into the church. We had left strict instructions with the ushers that latecomers not be admitted under any circumstances, probably reflecting my adverse reaction to tardy arrivals at the Malcolm wedding. Bill Wells followed these instructions to the letter and locked the doors as the wedding began. This kept Marian Clubb, wife of the U.S. Consul General, from getting in for the ceremony, but she graciously stayed around to wish us well anyway.

After shaking hands and chatting with the guests, signing the church marriage certificate with the maid of honor, best man, and clergymen as witnesses, and having one last round of wedding party pictures taken, Lyn and I, Dorie and Sam, were driven to the reception. It was a good party. Our instincts about its composition were correct, and as the reception wore on I met many of Lyn's friends for the first time, young people who had come to Peip'ing after I left it the previous September. There were toasts, "finger food" of tasty North Chinese specialties to eat, and a wedding cake to cut. By the time it was dark outside the party was well launched on what would be a protracted evening of celebration, and we could properly take our leave. Mrs. Shaw had passed the word that rice should not be tossed at us when we left because that would be unseemly amid the hunger conditions in China, but a few either did not hear this, or did not care.

Some rice flew anyway as we ran to the waiting Stanvac car for the short trip to our new home.

Once there we found Pien had prepared a full steak dinner for us, served in the little dining room that was lighted only with candles. I suppose the dinner was delicious, at least it looked good, but neither of us was hungry and we only picked at the food on our plates. I had managed to bring along some champagne from the reception, which we sipped offering toasts to each other and to ourselves. And finally, when the table had been cleared and we were sitting in candlelight with coffee and the last of our champagne, I got up and walked to Lyn's place, taking her wedding gift from my pocket as a I went. The gift was a small strand of pearls, bought at a store in the old Chinese City earlier in the week. I remember my hands trembling as I fastened the clasp at Lyn's neck, and I am sure my eyes were misty, for it was a very special and emotional moment. We were now actually married, and all the waiting and wondering and agonizing about it was behind us.

Peip'ing, Late Spring 1948

The honeymoon, short as it was, passed quickly and happily in our new house. An unexpected event occurred the second night, however, about one or two in the morning. We were both fast asleep when Lyn gave me a nudge and whispered she thought she heard someone in the house. I was skeptical, of course, remembering from somewhere that new brides were prone to hear strange noises in the night. Reluctantly, I roused myself and sleepily groped for a robe, making as much noise as possible in the process. Just as I was parting the curtain that separated our bed from the sitting room there came a loud crash from the dining room, followed by the sound of a door closing hastily. I called loudly for Pien to come and turned on the lights.

There on floor, next to one of the dining room chests, was a broken plate and some cookie crumbs. The plate had been perched on top of the chest, and must have been brushed off by the intruder. Maybe he was even stopping to sample the cookies when it happened. In any case, this was the noise Lyn had heard, and it confirmed that someone had been in the house looking for something to take away. There was no point in calling the police. Nothing had been taken, and there was no way to identify the intruder, who was certainly far away by the time we discovered the intrusion. Pien told us there was a recognized routine in these situations. If the householder hears a thief and gives nominal chase, the robber leaves and does no harm. If no one awakens, of course, the thief has a free hand.

And then it was Tuesday morning, the real world reappeared, and it was time for Lyn to leave for school. I had nothing to do, knew very few people in Peip'ing, and those I did know were all at work somewhere. A bit of lazy idleness is fine every now and then, and I am usually glad to take advantage of it, but by that day's end the inactivity and isolation in the house had become incredibly boring. Two months or so of waiting in Peip'ing yawned bleakly ahead of me. Happily, it did not last long.

The next day I received word from Jim Hunter, Regional Director of the CRM in Peip'ing, saying he wished to see me. When I met him later in his office, he told me the Shanghai interview had gone well, and he now had approval to hire me for a job that would start on April 12th and continue until the end of June. This was truly a major break. At one stroke, so to speak, the problem of my boredom and inaction was solved, and on top of that we would be adding an unexpected $350 a month, in salary and living allowances, to our meager resources. I was so elated I practically whooped aloud all the way home with the good news.

At the end of the war with the Axis powers, a major effort to repair some of the war's damage was mounted under the auspices of the United Nations. Termed the "United Nations Relief and Rehabilitation Administration" (UNRRA), it was worldwide in coverage. In China, the UNRRA program ultimately procured and distributed US$658 million in food, clothing, medical supplies, and material for agricultural and industrial rehabilitation. The U.S. government's contribution was approximately 72 percent of this total, or around US$474 million.

As the UNRRA program was winding down, Congress passed a U.S. Foreign Relief Program in May of 1947 (Public Law 84). China's allocation under this program was essentially a supplemental effort to continue UNRRA-type relief until mid-1948, by which time the law would expire and China's situation and needs could be further assessed. The CRM organization I was now joining was the responsible agency in China for this Foreign Relief Program. CRM eventually distributed over US$48 million worth of cereals, seeds, pesticides, and medical supplies, and supported a number of special projects financed from a special local currency account. These sums do not seem large now, but in those days they represented a significant effort to relieve immediate post-war human need.

The economic picture in China in early 1948 was as unrelievedly grim as the Nationalist military situation. The inflation, which started during the war with Japan, continued at higher and higher rates as government deficits went unchecked, fueled now by military and other expenditures arising from the civil war. Plant equipment and infrastructure of all kinds were badly run down; foreign trade was stagnant; domestic industry never recovered from the war's disrupting and destroying impact. People in the countryside resorted to barter to meet their consumption requirements, and tended to hoard stocks of basic foodstuffs. But people in the cities, dependent on wages and salaries, could not keep pace with the inflation or defend themselves in the same way. When city dwellers had to barter it meant giving up things permanently, household goods and prized family possessions, not reproducible farm items such as vegetables and poultry.

Widespread corruption at all levels, governmental and private, exacerbated the economic distress, as did insecurity arising from piracy and robbery such as I had experienced in the south. Any organization structured and financed as was the CRM could not correct all these problems in the midst of civil war, and particularly one going badly for the Nationalists. But the hope was that it might, in the words of a U.S. government report, "...assist in retarding the current economic deterioration."

The CRM office in Peip'ing was quite small, and included about half a dozen Americans. All were associated in some way on a temporary basis, as I was, and were not foreign service professionals. Even the Director, who had been for many years a missionary in Peip'ing, was not a career foreign service officer. The staff also included several secretaries and administrative people who were locally hired and came from diverse backgrounds — Anglo-Chinese, White Russian exiles, and Jewish refugees from Europe. An equal number of Chinese acted as interpreters and translators, accompanying the Americans on their rounds.

CRM was housed in a large compound at the eastern end of Legation Street, but used only a small part of it. The compound included godown [warehouse] space used to store relief supplies, and sheds where vehicles were kept. Except for the Director and the administrative officer, no one had a private office. The rest of us had desks in large rooms where the constant coming and going of others was a distraction, but where gossiping and protracted passing the time of day were also endemic.

My responsibilities were to inspect medical and welfare projects that had received relief grants from CRM, tracking their periodic progress and making completion reports, with recommendations, when the grants had run out. In other cases, where projects had applied for grants, I would investigate the proposals to determine whether they were eligible for assistance, and whether the project had merit. Finally, from time to time, I was expected to write a report for the main office in Shanghai on local (i.e., Peip'ing) economic and political conditions. Presumably, whatever I wrote was added to the mass of data coming from U.S. consular, military and relief offices all over China, to be sifted and weighed by those responsible for shaping U.S. policies toward China during that rapidly changing, and very difficult, period.

In the course of my duties with CRM I paid a visit to, among other places, the main Chinese prison in Peip'ing. I went there in the company of two missionary doctors who visited the place about once a week, and did what they could to alleviate the suffering of seriously ill prisoners. The doctors were not allowed to treat patients, but they could change bandages, apply medications, and distribute aspirin and other stopgap palliatives. Many prisoners had lost legs or arms, or parts of them, to tuberculosis, and these received fresh bandages and dressings for their stumps. The doctors assured me I was in no danger of getting TB because the contact with prisoners was so fleeting, and I was probably already immune, but the sight of these patients was a shock and I was always uneasy after these visits. Although conditions in the prison were unquestionably poor, and nothing I would willingly undergo, they were not as totally bad as I expected them to be.

Another interesting project supported by CRM was a boys' orphanage, run by Belgian priests in a northern corner of the city. The orphanage was situated on a small parcel of waste land donated by a Chinese landowner, and there boys and priests together built dormitories and school rooms from scrap materials salvaged here and there. The priests shared the food and lodging available for the boys, and taught them basic reading and writing plus craft/artisan skills. These skills were then used to make items for sale, or to allow some boys to become gainfully employed, and proceeds from these activities were used to help run the place.

A China Story: From Peip'ing to Beijing

The boys came from the streets, abandoned, lost or orphaned, living by their wits and begging when the priests found them. They were offered a chance to take part in a joint venture if they agreed to abide by the rules, and accepting the rules offered a genuine chance to make a new life. If boys refused the offer, and some did, one hated to think what probably became of them. The modest and practical approach of the project was very hopeful and exciting, but it called for enormous dedication on the part of the priests.

The projects I dealt with for CRM all involved some medical or social problem, many of them providing assistance to the handicapped or schooling for those unlikely to receive it through regular facilities. In the course of the next two months I managed to see a wide variety of such activities, and was surprised to find there was still much altruism in a society that was also cruel and indifferent to people in so many ways. My new job also let me observe life in the back streets and crowded residential areas in and around Peip'ing, an experience that both tugged at my conscience and repelled me. The squalor and misery that existed in some of those places was, to me, simply unbelievable.

Once I started working again, our lives as a married couple fell into a new routine. We left for work/school in the morning and returned in the afternoon, with weekends for play. Many newcomers had arrived in Peip'ing in recent months to study some aspect of Chinese language or culture under Fulbright or other grants. Our social life was increasingly linked with people from this group rather than the oil company classmen, most of whom had by then completed their language training and departed for their regular assignments. One couple we came to know well was the Boormans, Howie and Maggie.

The Boormans had married in Shanghai, a week before our wedding, and this gave us a strong bond in common from the start. Howie, a Foreign Service officer, was a student in the State Department's language school, an intensive program aimed at producing complete fluency in both written and spoken Chinese in about two years. Howie had studied Japanese in the Navy's wartime language school in Boulder, Colorado, and was therefore not a complete stranger to Asian languages. Maggie had been married previously to another Foreign Service officer, and had served in Chungking during the war with Japan. Now back in China, and married to Howie, she was also a teacher at PAS. The four of us thus had in common not only our recent marriages, but similar backgrounds in

Japanese language and being faculty colleagues in PAS. Through the Boormans we came to meet other people in the language school and in the Foreign Service.

One of the Fulbright students, an anthropologist named Frank Besaac, was studying Mongolian language and culture. Frank was something of a loner, living in the northern part of the Tartar City, but he had become a part of the group that met socially in the Fang Chia Yuan compound during the time I was in Canton. At one point, in the course of his study of things Mongolian, he had managed to meet the Soderbom brothers. These were two Swedish nationals who had first come to inner Asia with the famous Swedish explorer, Sven Hedin, when he made his extensive journeys into Mongolia in the 1920s and 30s. The Soderboms had stayed in Asia after that, and during the war with Japan they were suspected of being spies for the Japanese, then double agents for the Chinese, and even triple agents for the British or Americans. Frank thought we would find them interesting, and wanted to arrange an opportunity for us to meet them. After some negotiation one of the brothers, whose name was George, finally agreed to come with Frank to our house for dinner.

George Soderbom was a huge man, bearded but largely bald on the top of his head, and unkempt in dress and appearance. He ate dinner with obvious relish and considerable noise, belching loudly and often in the course of the meal. When our meal ended, we adjourned to the small sitting room for coffee. The night was hot. No breeze came through the open doors to the courtyard, and for a long time there was no electricity. This happened often in Peip'ing, as it had in Canton. Reasons for the lapses could be almost anything, but probably were due mostly to the worn out and faulty equipment in the systems.

In the candlelit gloom, the perspiration stood out on George Soderbom's forehead, adding a sinister touch to his brooding hulk crammed into a chair clearly way too small for him. Having eaten well he kept falling asleep, and his heavy breathing was interrupted now and then by soft snoring sounds. We chatted away with Frank, but our chief guest clearly was not interested in holding up his part of any conversation. Watching Soderbom as he dozed, and in the heat and half light of the room, one could easily imagine him as a shadowy figure, heavily involved in all sorts of Asian intrigue. He was perfectly typecast for it, but he was not about to give us any insights into his reputedly exciting life of espionage and adventure. After an hour or so of vainly waiting for George to wake up and join the party,

A China Story: From Peip'ing to Beijing

Frank roused him and they left. This had been an evening rich in possibilities, but arid as the Gobi Desert when it came to actual content.

Another unusual evening came along about the same time. Someone we knew, probably Frank Besaac again, asked if we would like to meet a group of three young people who were stopping in Peip'ing on their way overland to India through central Asia and Tibet. Two were Americans, a man and woman. The man was Faubion Bowers, who had been aide-de-camp and personal interpreter to Gen. MacArthur during the early period of the Japanese Occupation. The third person was an Indian woman named Santha Rama Rau who, though still in her twenties, had already published one well-received novel. The journey on which they were embarked sounded like high adventure, albeit risky, and we again agreed this could be an interesting evening. In short order, Frank appeared with the three in tow for dinner.

Miss Rau's manners were a considerable improvement over George Soderbom's, and she entered into conversation with great zest. She arrived dressed elegantly in a brocaded sari, her arms weighted heavily with gold bangles. Unfortunately, she also had the haughty, more than slightly condescending, air that well-born, rich, educated people from the sub-continent often carried in those final days of the British Raj, and in some cases still do.

The evening's chatter dealt largely with what was then happening in China. Miss Rau was scathing in her comments on the Nationalist government, and confident to the point of certainty that the Communists would win and bring badly needed change to the countryside. Of course, she observed, there would have to be wholesale elimination of the landed and wealthy classes in China, but this was essential for any true reforms to take place. When someone asked if this would be necessary in her homeland, India, as well, she replied that an equally thorough housecleaning of the elite groups there was inevitable. And when queried still further whether this would mean danger for her own family, who were rich and socially well-placed, she blandly agreed and added they would deserve whatever they received. The cold disdain with which Miss Rau dismissed the possible demise of her family and its class in some revolutionary upheaval struck us as incredibly callous. But, as we later discussed the evening among ourselves, we doubted she would be anywhere near the scene if it ever came to pass.

For the most part, however, our socializing was in groups of young people working and studying in Peip'ing. As was true the previous summer, and in Canton, these were non-Chinese, mostly Americans. Chinese were not consciously excluded from these social occasions, but it remained difficult to meet Chinese who were comfortable with the casual partying, whether due to language shortcomings (on both sides) or unease at the informality that prevailed.

Half the students in Lyn's classes were Chinese, of course, and some of them would drop by the house in the afternoon after school, but this was part of a teacher/student relationship. A teacher had a very special place in Chinese society, respected, almost revered in some cases, and therefore somewhat aloof from others. Students would never expect to meet with their teachers on the basis of coming together as social equals. My relations with the interpreters in the CRM office were cordial and pleasant, but they would be reluctant to accept, say, an invitation to dinner because they would feel obligated to reciprocate in some way. This could be embarrassing if they lived in poor surroundings, as many did, or more expensive than they could afford if they felt obliged to take us to dinner in a restaurant. One knew better than to take the initiative in these cases because sensitivities (another word for "face") were involved. So there was an invisible line of sorts, an unspoken barrier, that kept Chinese and non-Chinese apart in the casual social life that flourished, and this limited our contacts with Chinese to official parties, or the world of work and school.

We found ourselves very busy that Spring. There were dinner parties, sometimes at restaurants in the old city, and occasional excursions into the countryside whenever it was reportedly safe to venture outside the city walls. As the weather grew warmer there were tennis and swimming, and much casual dropping in on people, or being dropped in on, for tea or a drink on a weekend afternoon. My new status as husband of a faculty member also brought me the role of chaperone at PAS dances and parties, a task I performed reluctantly and with ill grace.

Conversation at these social gatherings was lively and informed, and more likely to deal with the current political/military situation than, say, the conversations I knew from Stanvac parties in Canton. Lyn and I had always been conscious that something was unreal about the easygoing and seemingly normal lives we led, and we were always aware, dimly perhaps and somewhere off the horizon, that forceful and violent changes were taking place in China. As Spring moved toward Summer, we sensed that the struggle in China was grinding toward a resolution, but that still seemed a long time away and we felt no sense of urgency about our own situation.

Wedding vows — Reverend Shaw and Easton officiating

Bride and groom greeting guests

Lyn and Jim at the reception

CHAPTER ELEVEN

"The measure of China's tragedy is not Shanghai's roaring inflation, nor the tide of battles lost & won. It is the horde of refugees streaming southward, 30,000,000 starving, diseased, despairing people. They stand for the breakdown of Chinese society under Communist hammer blows which caught China in the difficult and disturbing transition toward Western progress."

Time, Vol. LI I, No. 4, July 26, 1948, p. 23.

"CHINESE INFLATION SOARS TO NEW PEAK - CURRENCY REACHES 4 MILLION TO ONE U.S. DOLLAR - PRICE LEVELS ALSO SPIRAL UP"

New York Times, June 26, 1948, p. 7.

Peip'ing, Summer 1948

But an urgency did come in one sense, and very soon. One day late in May Lyn told me she had been to visit an obstetrician at the Peking Union Medical College (PUMC) hospital, the outcome of which was confirmation that Lyn was pregnant. We had not planned to have a child until we were back in the States and settled into some solvent, stable situation, but we had also been pretty casual about practicing birth control. I think we felt it could not happen to us, but now we were faced with proof that it could and it produced multiple sensations. There was pleasure, disbelief, wonder, pride, mild panic and a strong sense of embarrassment that a couple married such a short time would produce a child. We could almost see the fingers being counted when the news reached families in the States. The one offsetting factor was the discovery, soon thereafter, that the Boormans were in the same boat. Both offspring were expected about the same time, late January in the new year, and Lyn and Maggie would share the experiences of impending motherhood in tandem, so to speak.

At about the same time, there was change brewing in CRM where I worked. Although the CRM itself was slated to close at the end of June, when the Public Law creating it expired, the Foreign Assistance Act of 1948, known popularly as the "Marshall Plan," was coming into being. While essentially designed to provide funding for the reconstruction of war-ravaged Europe, Title IV of the Marshall Plan, called the "China Aid Act of 1948", also authorized expenditure of US$338 million for economic assistance to China, of which a total of US$275 million was appropriated for use in 1948-9. The Agency administering these aid programs was called the "Economic Cooperation Administration" (ECA), and the Chief of the ECA Mission to China, Roger D. Lapham, arrived to take up his post in Shanghai the first week in June. The formal Economic Aid Agreement between China and the U.S. was signed on July 3rd, 1948.

The ECA program itself called for three kinds of activities: provision of basic commodities (food, fuel, cotton, fertilizer and coal), initiation of industrial reconstruction and replacement measures, and formation and support of a Joint Commission on Rural Reconstruction in China (JCRR). To get things moving as quickly as possible, ECA was to take over and adapt to its new purposes the existing CRM agency. This meant continuing some of CRM's activities of a relief nature, and using locally recruited Americans, local non-American staff, private firms and voluntary relief agencies as widely as possible. For the American staff in CRM's Peip'ing office, who thought their appointments would end in June, there now came an unexpected opportunity to stay involved with relief efforts. If we wanted them, there would be positions available in the new and expanded U.S. aid program about to get under way.

One of these new activities would be a program of food distribution that would operate through a civilian rationing system in urban areas. Basic foodstuffs, flour in the case of Peip'ing but rice in other parts of China, would be sold through designated ration shops, and at fixed prices, against ration coupons issued to all registered city dwellers. In the inflationary environment that existed, when the prices of all other commodities were rising rapidly, this amounted to a subsidized basic food supply.

A China Story: From Peip'ing to Beijing

The position I was offered, if we agreed to stay on in Peip'ing, was titled "Assistant Food Rationing Officer." This would involve supervising the Chinese staff who inspected the ration shops and warehouses, maintaining the accounts of the commodities being distributed in Peip'ing, ordering new supplies to insure timely delivery, and filing periodic reports on stock positions and currency receipts. The job carried a rating as Foreign Service Staff Officer, Grade 9, an annual salary of US$3960 plus living allowances, and return passage to the States for the appointee and dependents when the assignment ended. The salary was equal to what I had been earning with Stanvac, and the living allowances were also comparable.

Lyn and I methodically worked our way to a decision whether to stay on, carefully weighing both sides. Against taking the ECA offer were some obvious and powerful negative considerations. For one thing, we had planned all along to leave China by the end of June and start searching seriously for new career possibilities back in the States. Taking the ECA job would not change that broad objective, only delay getting around to it. A second factor was that China was a hazardous place, and no one could be certain what would happen over the next few months, or what kinds of specific dangers might materialize. And finally, we now had an unborn child to think about, and whether staying in Peip'ing would pose serious risk to Lyn and the baby.

On the other hand, we could think of reasons, or maybe they were rationalizations, why it might be a good idea to accept the ECA offer. The first involved the question of danger from the civil war then heating up. We had become inured to conditions in China over the period we both had spent there. While things were undoubtedly going on, many of them very nasty, foreigners, and particularly Americans, seemed to escape any serious harm. The Canton riot was scary, for example, but no one was actually killed. One was more likely to be killed in an automobile accident back home, we told ourselves, than be hurt as a side effect of the hostilities in China. The ECA job would give me the status of an employee of the U.S. Government, with dependents, and that entailed extra protection and support not available to private citizens abroad; special efforts would probably be made to spirit us out of any danger. But beyond that, we doubted the Chinese, Nationalist or Communist, would let anything serious happen to lovely Peip'ing, a crown jewel in their national cultural heritage.

When we turned our thoughts to the baby, we felt quite confident. The staff and facilities at Peking Union Medical College (PUMC), the Rockefeller-endowed teaching hospital, were excellent. Lyn would receive pre-natal care there, and this is where the baby would be born. The obstetrician who would be in charge, Dr. Khati Lim, was a 1929 graduate of PUMC, one of the first woman doctors in China, and the first Chinese woman to receive graduate medical instruction abroad, at the University of Edinburgh. If anything, the care of mother and baby would be superior to what they would receive in the States as dependents of someone unemployed and having trouble finding a new job.

From a financial point of the view, the ECA offer looked very attractive, as though we had stayed with Stanvac after all. Our limited experience as a married couple indicated that two could live comfortably and quite cheaply in Peip'ing, and the jump in salary (to nearly twice what I was getting with CRM) would enable us to save a sizable amount for our eventual return home. Payment of our way back to the States, along with any household goods we wished to ship, was frosting on the cake in the sense that such expense would no longer come out of our pockets.

Finally, we had grown to like our life in Peip'ing. The people we knew were congenial and fun, and as a group much more interesting than the oil company classmen. CRM was not the all-consuming employer Stanvac had been, and we expected that ECA would be equally undemanding of our private lives and time. Lyn was not certain she wanted to teach at PAS in the Fall, but if she did Alice Moore was returning as principal and the situation there could only improve. There was also the fact that we would probably be witnesses to a major historic event; there was little doubt in our minds that Communist forces would soon prevail in North China. If anything, given the discounting we had already given the risk factors, this chance to observe at first hand a change in Chinese dynasties added excitement to the opportunity to stay on in China. Putting all together, the decision to accept the ECA position was not hard to reach, and we had few serious doubts this was a good decision.

The PAS held its 1948 graduation on June 7th, following a Field Day in mid-May, a school picnic at the Jade Fountain Pagoda, and a Junior Prom in honor of the Senior Class. Given the uncertainties looming ahead, this was a remarkably "normal" and upbeat set of celebrations. Shortly after school closed, however, an unpleasant set of circumstances came to light. The Treasurer of the school board, albeit acting somewhat late in the year, discovered serious discrepancies between the amounts of money held in the school's safe and the amounts supposed to have been collected in tuition fees in January.

Lyn had refused to have any part in the money affairs of the school during the period when Ruth was acting as principal, recalling only too vividly her earlier bitter personal experience with Ruth over personal finances. On at least one occasion Lyn had noticed IOUs from PAS faculty members in the school's safe, placed there to cover amounts they had withdrawn from it. Investigation of the losses by Ernest Shaw and some of the other Board members failed to uncover any legitimate explanation for these withdrawals, and they were also unable to establish the full amount of the losses.

In the end, Ruth and the person acting as school secretary were allowed to resign and leave Peip'ing, and the matter was not publicized. Whether the losses were due to peculation or just sloppy administration, Ruth was the one in charge and therefore responsible. Her departure was no loss to us, nor to the school; for my part, the manner of her departure was full vindication of the suspicions I had of her all along.

With the change from CRM to ECA there also came a change in directors. Jim Hunter, who had hired me, was ready to return to the States with his family. He was replaced by Ritchie Davis, a professor at the University of Indiana's School of Law, who was on leave from the university to take the ECA appointment. Ritchie, recently divorced and then in his early to mid-forties, was born in Peip'ing and came from a Methodist missionary family. He spoke fluent Chinese, and still had some contacts among both the foreign and Chinese communities. Ritchie was somewhat heavy set, and at first we found him reserved, even gruff in manner, rather like the fictional detective character Nero Wolf. As he settled into his new position this impression changed considerably. Ritchie was, in reality, a gentle man with a good sense of humor, a keen analytical mind, a large store of experience and background, and an ability to make difficult decisions readily. He was sensitive to the needs of the ECA staff, American and non-American alike, and an excellent administrator. I quickly came to appreciate the good fortune that brought Ritchie to Peip'ing, a demanding supervisor but fair, understanding, and highly likable.

Having decided to stay on with ECA, and with the PAS school term ended, Lyn and I began to think about finding new quarters. The short-term lease on our compound on Hsi Tsung Pu hut'ung was due to end by the first of July. Although it was certainly an adequate arrangement, we thought it wise to look for something better before signing an extension of the lease. We put out word we were house hunting and quickly came across what, to us, was an absolutely perfect solution. The friend of a colleague at ECA owned a little house in Peip'ing, furnished and refurbished as a place to retire some day. The friend, who was stationed with the Hong Kong Shanghai Bank in Shanghai, was uneasy having a house sitting idle in a time of such great uncertainty, and thus ready to let it go to any responsible tenant for a pittance. One look at the house and we were completely taken with it.

Our new home, self-contained in its own little compound, was located just off Morrison Street, a few blocks north and west of the Tung An Market in an area called Nai Tse Fu. One entered the house from Feng Sheng hut'ung, and stepped into a small courtyard, complete with a flowering fruit tree. The main living quarters formed one side of the compound, and a small separate storeroom was located at the far end. A high wall, opposite the main building and running parallel to it, was the barrier to the outside world, maintaining the privacy and anonymity of the court and living quarters inside. All had been freshly painted — vermilion on the window frames and columns, and green, red and gold characters on the ends of the roof poles holding the ceramic tiled roof, also newly replaced.

Inside the main building was a living/dining area, perhaps thirty feet long and twelve feet wide, at one end of which was a tiny bedroom and bath. At the other end of this large room were the kitchen and the servants' quarters, only slightly larger than the bedroom and bath. The living room contained two lovely brass-fitted chests that faced anyone entering from the court outside; hanging between them were "ancestor portraits," scrolls with paintings of an elderly Ch'ing Dynasty couple. Sofas and chairs were comfortable, and a coffee table and end tables complemented them; the dining table and chairs were in a traditional Chinese style and made of polished wood, and there was a handsome sideboard nearby.

The main thing one could say for the bedroom was that it afforded privacy because it had a door, something our Hsi Tsung Pu compound did not have. The bedroom had barely enough room for a double bed, an armoire, and a camphor chest. The living room part was heated by a small pot-bellied, coal-burning stove that stood in a corner between a sofa and an easy chair; the dining part of the room was next to the kitchen, and received heat from the coal-burning cooking stove located there; the bedroom was unheated. The separate store room in the courtyard was empty, but we had so few belongings of our own there was no immediate need for it. Eventually, we used it to store our coal supply for the winter. The kitchen and servants' quarters were far superior to those at Hsi Tsung Pu, both in size and in equipment, and Pien and Ho seemed as delighted as we with the new quarters. The freshness and color of the newly painted exterior, and the good taste of the interior furnishings, were simply stunning compared with the drabness of our former compound. We moved as soon as we could, and settled in comfortably in the blink of an eye. School was over for Lyn, and I was now the one who left each morning for work, leaving Lyn alone in the new house. But it was not long before that changed.

Helen Beaumont, one of the Ferguson sisters whom Lyn and I had met the previous summer, was then running the Marco Polo Shop, an up-scale boutique selling Chinese furniture and art work in the Legation Quarter. The store was owned by a man named Arthur Porter, but he was rarely in it and left management of the place largely to Helen. Business was not particularly brisk at the time. Visitors to Peip'ing who had money, but neither the time nor inclination to browse through the shops in the Chinese city, could find nice things at the Marco Polo, though no bargains. Helen asked if Lyn would like to help out in the store. This was more a matter of having someone around as good company than anything else. The hours were not onerous, and the work light and agreeable for someone in the early stages of pregnancy. The pay, of course, was minimal.

Lyn gladly accepted Helen's offer, and we both were again employed. We returned home for lunch each day, that being the usual practice for foreigners, and went back to our respective work places for the afternoons. A satisfying existence we had, comfortable in our new surroundings, enjoying people we knew and with whom we worked, and once again at some financial ease. I was gradually learning a new set of ropes in connection with the ECA job, and for the moment things were turning out very well for us.

The mechanics of the ration program were put in place by city government officials, subject to approval and oversight by ECA, and the program went into effect rather quickly. Ration shops were designated, ration coupons printed and issued to all residents of the city, flour supplies began arriving and were distributed to the shops, and people were getting access to a basic ration of flour based on the size and composition of families. I travelled around the city with the three Chinese inspectors locally hired by ECA, each of whom had a different part of the city to cover. Together we checked the books of the ration shops to ensure they tallied with the coupons on hand and the supplies remaining. We also inspected the physical condition of the flour held in the shops, and tried to be present when flour was actually distributed to observe how the process worked

Although almost everything in China in those days was tinged with graft, or "squeeze" as it was often called, the ration program seemed to operate in honest and open fashion for the most part. We probably would have heard if people were being cheated out of their rations, for the program was highly publicized and very popular. Lack of serious complaints was taken, and probably rightly, as a sign that the program was largely meeting its objectives.

In mid-July Lyn went to PUMC for a regular pre-natal check-up. She had not been feeling well, but that was not the reason for the visit to the doctor. After examining her, Dr. Lim ordered her into a hospital bed immediately and told her she would remain under observation for an unspecified period. I was informed at work, and asked to bring Lyn's personal effects to the hospital as soon as possible. The reason for the drastic action was infectious hepatitis. This was not uncommon in China, given the prevailing sanitation conditions everywhere. For the most part the illness was dismissed as "yellow jaundice," considered a rather comical malady because it turned non-Chinese people yellow. To me, it was surprising that Dr. Lim should take Lyn's condition so seriously. As I was to learn from Dr. Lim, however, because Lyn was pregnant there was danger she might abort the child. Should this occur, the hepatitis would make it very difficult to control the loss of blood, thus posing great risk to Lyn.

Considerably sobered and chastened at this news, I anxiously watched Lyn's progress over the next few days. Happily, she soon began to feel better, and at the end of ten days Dr. Lim decided she was well enough to be released and return home. The job at the Marco Polo Shop ended then and there, replaced by a period of extended convalescence in our new quarters. Since she could not eat fats, feeding Lyn became an unwelcome challenge to the cook, who normally prepared all meals in large amounts of cooking oil. The solution was a diet for both of us that was bland and fat-free, but Pien was clearly unhappy to be serving us things he believed unworthy of his best, tastiest, and most fattening efforts. There was also a ban on alcohol consumption by Lyn, at least for six months. This could have been a blessing in disguise, however, since subsequent medical research indicates that alcohol taken during pregnancy can have harmful side effects on the unborn child.

During this period of resting and convalescence we came to really appreciate our new living quarters. Peip'ing can be hot in the summer, but mornings were often cool and pleasant. Even at mid-day the weather was usually only comfortably warm. We now took meals in our courtyard, under the shade of the fruit tree, and from that vantage point we could hear the street sounds of the hut'ung, particularly in the mornings at breakfast time.

Because Peip'ing compounds were sealed off from the hut'ung lanes by high walls, without windows, there was no way to see who was passing by in the hut'ung short of standing at an open gate. Itinerant vendors of all kinds made their presence known by making some distinguishable noise to alert potential customers within the compounds. A particular, recognizable sound came from each — the man selling vegetables, the barber, the fish monger, the rag picker, the fortune teller, the hot noodle seller, the bean curd man, the candled fruit seller and many, many others. Some carried small hand clappers on which they struck a special rhythm, some used gongs of differing sizes and tones, some had horns, some played a stringed instrument, some had small drums, and some simply repeated a shouted announcement of what they were selling. When householders heard the approach of a hawker selling some good or service they wanted, they would open the door to the hut'ung and flag him down.

All through the day the sounds of this passing parade came over the walls, a cacophony of commerce. Since we did not have to learn who was selling what, that being Pien's job, we came to distinguish only a few of the sounds, but it was a constant treat for us to sit in our little court and listen to the clicks, bongs, rattles, toots, tinkles and shouts that passed outside our wall.

By mid-August Lyn had pretty well recovered from the hepatitis, the pregnancy was proceeding satisfactorily, and she felt well again. The Boormans suggested that we travel together out into the Western Hills to spend a weekend at a small hotel still operating there. Howie had determined, through his State Department contacts, that the military situation in the area around Peip'ing was relatively quiet for the time being, and unlikely to pose any problems from roving Communist patrols. There now being no medical reason to hold us back, we agreed to accompany the Boormans.

Howie arranged for the transport, and one sunny Saturday morning he and Maggie appeared in a battered old touring car of indeterminate make, dating from the late 1920s or early 1930s, with two Chinese in charge of operations. There was some trouble getting the car to start when we set out from our house, and there were a couple of unscheduled stops in traffic before we even left the city walls, but eventually we were out of the city and into the countryside. The stalling continued, however, and eventually called for special action on the part of our Chinese crew. One of them positioned himself on the right front fender, the hood propped up, and by keeping his hand on some part of the engine (which we could not see from where we sat) was able to keep the motor running. From time to time, though, the engine would heat up and the man on the fender would leap off, seize a small pail that was kept on the front seat, fill it with water from a nearby ditch, and throw the water on the steaming engine. For some reason this did not crack the engine block, but did seem to cool it down a bit, and so we progressed until we finally reached our destination.

Once there, we dismissed our drivers after obtaining their promise to take us back to Peip'ing the following afternoon. We had little confidence they could make it back in that car, but we had no obvious alternative. The hotel rooms were pretty grim, evidence that business had not been good for a long time, though the proprietors were doing their best merely to keep afloat. The four of us were the only guests that weekend. The beds were lumpy, the springs creaked, the floors and furnishings were none too clean, and when I lifted the water basin from the dresser there was a dead scorpion underneath. Having unpacked to an extent that seemed prudent, considering the surroundings, we gathered on a small patio to look out over the countryside, eventually have dinner there, and then watch the sun set over the Western Hills. All was very rural, very quiet, and very lovely, and because the Boormans were always good company we thoroughly enjoyed the evening.

The next day the car and drivers arrived as promised and we returned to Peip'ing. The two must have done some repair work on the car overnight because the drive back was uneventful, with no intermittent stops to cool off the engine. All in all, the weekend proved a nice change of pace for us, and in surroundings so peaceful the civil war seemed very, very far away.

CHAPTER TWELVE

"[The conduct of the civil war] is a gloomy picture and one would expect the government to clutch at any means of improving the situation. Nevertheless it ignores competent military advice and fails to take advantage of military opportunities offered. This is due in large part to the fact that government and military leadership continue to deteriorate as the Generalissimo selects men on the basis of personal reliability rather than military competence."

Letter from Ambassador in China to Secretary Marshall, dated August 10, 1948, reprinted in United States Relations with China, p. 885.

"TSINAN IS CAPTURED BY CHINESE COMMUNISTS; TROOP REVOLTS SPED SHANTUNG CAPITAL'S FALL"

New York Times, September 25, 1948, p. 6.

Peip'ing, Late Summer/Early Fall 1948

With the passage of summer and the onset of autumn, there was a tangible change in the atmosphere in Peip'ing. The sense that time was running out on the Nationalist government became more acute, the expectation that things would soon come to a head became more pronounced. Evidence of disintegration was everywhere. In a desperate move to shore up the faltering economy, the Nationalists announced a currency reform on August 19th. This involved creation of a new monetary unit, the Gold Yuan, allegedly backed with gold and exchangeable for the old inflated currency at a rate of GY $1 equal to CN $3,000,000. The official foreign exchange rate for the new Gold Yuan, in turn, was set at GY

139

$4 equal to US $1. As officials of a U.S. government agency, ECA employees were expected to show support for the monetary reform effort by refraining from exchanging money anywhere but at the banks. We all did so for a while, and the reform remained fairly stable for about a month. After that the inflation resumed, as it was bound to do, and exchanging money at the official rate became increasingly costly for us. Eventually we dropped all pretense of supporting the reform, and went back to the streets to exchange money.

The gold backing for the new currency was something of a farce. Gold Yuan paper currency could not be exchanged for gold, as required in any monetary standard backed by a precious metal. Under the pressure of the Nationalist government's need for funds, with 80-90 percent of the budget going for war-related expenses, increases in paper money supplies were not constrained by the amount of gold held by the Nationalist Treasury. By mid-September prices of goods in the markets had doubled, and at one point merchants closed their stalls rather than pretend they were doing business at official ceiling prices. Large, anxious crowds milled around the ration shops when they were open for distribution of ECA-provided flour at official prices, but the supplies were maintained and the ration system continued to function. By the middle of October, the original note issue of GY$2 billion had already been increased to GY$9 billion.

The military situation was also moving rapidly against the Nationalist cause. The capital of Shantung Province, Tsinan, fell to Communist forces on September 23-24, and with its loss the large area east and south of Peip'ing passed into Communist control. According to reports from the U.S. Consul General in Tsingtao, which still remained in Nationalist hands, the factors accounting for the Nationalist defeat were failure of reinforcements to move aggressively to the support of the defenders, the defections of large numbers of Nationalist troops, and the unwillingness of others to stand and fight. Nationalist losses in casualties, prisoners and defections were in the range of 85-100,000 troops, and the Communists also acquired 50,000 rifles and considerable stocks of ammunition.

At about the same time, the Communist forces were positioning themselves to destroy the Nationalist hold on Manchuria. A key element in their strategy was to capture the city of Chinchow, an important supply base for Nationalist troops in Manchuria located along the route from T'ientsin to Mukden. Once again, reinforcements to bolster the defense of Chinchow were slow to move from Mukden to the north and Hulutao to the south, the latter being a nearby port through which new reinforcements were actually sent for the purpose. Government units defending Chinchow defected on October 15th, and the Communists occupied it. This time not only were stocks of rifles and ammunition captured, but also great quantities of stores stockpiled for the use of Government troops in Manchuria. The loss of Chinchow sealed the eventual loss of all Manchuria, with its 300,000 government troops, their arms, and all their supplies and equipment.

The students at Peip'ing's major universities, Tsinghua, Peita (Peip'ing University) and Yenching, were increasingly active and vocal in protesting the failures and mistakes of the Government. Authorities often acted harshly in trying to quell dissent of any kind, and in the process many non-Communist students, airing legitimate grievances, were literally driven into the Communist camp. I returned home from work one day to hear from Lyn about one such incident.

Through several of the people we had come to know in Peip'ing, Americans mostly who were in close contact with students at the universities, Lyn learned of a student protest march that was to take place on a certain day. The students marched into the city as scheduled (the universities being located outside the walls) and eventually reached a point where they suddenly faced a line of armed troops blocking any further movement forward. Other troops quickly appeared at the entrances to side streets on two other sides, effectively blocking escape in those directions as well. At that point the students stopped and sat down facing the troops ahead of them. Several of the Americans Lyn had trailed along with then stepped forward and sat down with the students in the front rank, by their action defying the soldiers to fire on them as well.

Lyn was watching all this from the vantage point of a compound wall to one side of the confrontation area. At some point in the impasse an officer gave the order for the troops to charge their rifles with ammunition, which they did with loud clicks as the rifle bolts shot the rounds home. Lyn later reported never had she heard a sound as loud in her life. But, as she watched, a gate in the wall where she was standing opened, and a Chinese man reached out for her arm and brusquely pulled her inside the compound. Lyn was obviously pregnant at this time, and the Chinese man proceeded to berate her in fluent English for her foolhardiness in placing herself in such a dangerous position. In all honesty, Lyn did not have a good reply for being there other than her intense interest in what was happening, and despite the tongue-lashing she got she was grateful to the man for his intervention. As was I, when I later heard about it.

Outside the compound wall, the situation quickly changed. The students realized they were trapped with little opportunity to accomplish what they had set out to do, and slowly, reluctantly they turned and retraced their steps to their universities. The Americans also parted company and went their separate ways. On that day no one had been hurt, nothing was destroyed, and no tragedy ensued. This would come later, but the day's event was one more indication how rapidly the social and political fabrics were fraying.

The troop losses in Shantung and Manchuria spurred new government efforts to find replacements. Recruiting was carried out by a combination of neighborhood selection and press-gang methods, because there were no volunteers for an army that was so obviously losing the war. Young men of military age who could afford to pay a certain amount of money (usually negotiable) were released with a written statement saying they were exempt from military service. Most young men, not having the necessary amount of money to buy their way out, tried to stay out of sight. One day as I was driving about the city on my rounds of inspecting ration stores, I saw a long line of men, each tied to the man in front of him by a rope around the neck, shuffling along under armed guard. They were a dejected and sorry lot, and I asked the driver of the ECA jeep if these were Communist prisoners. No, was his reply, they were "hsin bing," that is, new soldiers. Recruits like this, once they reached an area of fighting, were defecting wholesale all over North China.

Although Lyn did not return to teach at PAS when school opened in September, she maintained contact with former colleagues and students. In the afternoons, small groups of students would often stop by the house to visit, sip tea, and hear Lyn's views on what was happening. These students were increasingly apprehensive about the future, and with good reason. They wondered what would happen to them and their families, since most came from relatively well-to-do homes, and they were concerned they might not get the U.S. college education for which PAS was preparing them. Some were already in contact with disaffected students at the local universities, and were beginning to reflect the political views current there. All felt more and more free, particularly in the safety of our house, to voice their disillusion and disappointment with the Nationalist government.

On one occasion, a very bright young PAS woman student was holding forth on some of the advantages that would come with a Communist victory. People, she said, would no longer have to eat the white flour that came from the greedy shopkeepers and landowners, but instead would happily eat coarse barley and millet grown by the sweat of an honest farmer's brow. Most people vastly preferred wheat flour to the coarse grains, and it was not clear whom she thought grew the wheat that went into the white flour, so in many ways hers was a naive comment. But the remark did capture some of the polarization of thought and revolutionary rhetoric that were becoming ever more openly expressed.

Peip'ing, Late Fall 1948

After the capture of Tsinan and Chinchow, General Chiang Kai Shek flew to Peip'ing to personally direct field operations in North China. Since he was miles from the areas where fighting was actually taking place, and there was little effective coordination of orders he gave, the result was complete confusion at the field level. Nationalist forces simply disintegrated, and the important Manchurian city of Changchun fell on October 20th, followed quickly by Mukden, which was surrendered on November 1st without a fight. After this Manchurian fiasco Chiang returned south to Nanking, in effect abandoning further efforts to retain North China.

The nominal commander of Nationalist forces in North China was General Fu Tso Yi, considered one of the best military commanders on the Nationalist side. He also had a reputation as a progressive and enlightened provincial war lord when compared to others. His troops were loyal to Fu Tso Yi, and were well trained and well motivated, but he was not one of the Generalissimo's favorites. As a result there was wide belief he was being shortchanged when receiving munitions and supplies from the central government. Toward the end of November, Communist forces succeeded in cutting off Fu Tso Yi's crack troops and isolating them in Inner Mongolia, after which his position in Peip'ing became hopeless. The Nationalist troops stationed there were not his own; they were from the south, and their ties and loyalties were to others. Such troops were in no way a match for the confident, and now well supplied, Communist forces converging on T'ientsin and Peip'ing.

The American Consulate General issued a circular on November 1st urging Americans to consider evacuation in light of the worsening military situation, and while normal transportation facilities were still available. Mission boards ordered their personnel to leave, many business people followed suit, and PAS closed its doors because several faculty members and students were about to go. Dorie Eldred was among these, and left for Tsingtao and eventual passage to the U.S. on November 16th. Seven of the fifteen Fulbright scholars in Peip'ing elected to go. Many Chinese, those with money and property, were also leaving, including the landlord of the first compound where Lyn lived on arrival in Peip'ing.

The local English language newspaper, the Peiping Chronicle, was still picturing daily events as minor aberrations in a world that still had the central government in full charge of everything. Rail traffic disruptions, shortages, losses of telephone service and the like were due to the work of "bandits," who were always about to be "mopped up" by government troops. The lengths to which the paper went to maintain this optimistic outlook were sometimes quite ludicrous. For example, the departure of the famous scholar, Dr. Hu Shih, which by some chance I happened to witness at the airport, was reported as no more than a quick visit to the south to look after some intellectual interests. From the looks of his baggage and the tenor of the farewells being offered him, however, he had not the faintest intention of returning.

The paper also interviewed the wife of one of the State Department language students as she waited for her departing flight at the Peip'ing airport. The reason she was leaving, the account said, was not because of the hostilities but because she was pregnant. If she had a son, the article continued, she wanted him to be born in the U.S. to make the boy eligible to become president some day.

As evacuation preparations advanced for many, foreigners and Chinese alike, Ritchie Davis called me into his office and asked if Lyn and I would volunteer to stay on through the Communist takeover. The decision had been made that ECA should retain a presence in China. If a rapprochement somehow came about with the Communists, and ECA continued its distribution of food and other relief supplies, then American staff would be needed to oversee this distribution.

A China Story: From Peip'ing to Beijing

Ritchie did not apply any pressure for us to stay, realizing that our situation was not the same as unattached Americans (of whom there were others on the ECA staff), but he did add that he hoped we would decide to stay.

Once again, we went over the arguments for and against staying in Peip'ing. They had not changed in any substantial respect from the last time we discussed them back in June, when we decided to take the ECA job. The reality of a Communist takeover was now much closer, but we still could not believe Peip'ing would be subjected to any drastic military action, and we doubted any physical harm would come to us. Reports filtering back from areas recently brought under Communist control, such as Tsinan, were encouraging. They claimed that foreigners were not being molested by the new regime, and were allowed to continue their missionary, teaching, medical and even business activities as before. Without too much deliberation, and without many misgivings, we decided to stay.

Our day-to-day lives at this point were still pretty much as usual. Inflation was raging, prices sometimes doubling or more in the course of a day, but we were paid in U.S. dollars, not Chinese currency. Converting dollars in small amounts only, to cover what would be needed for immediate purchases, it was possible to make ends meet without much difficulty. A couple of my efforts to economize had some unexpected consequences, though.

A colleague at ECA, who had lived in China for many years, told me he arranged to purchase coal for the winter at a favorable price, and offered to include a delivery to our house in the deal if we wished. I agreed, without having consulted with Pien, and the coal was duly delivered a few days later. Pien was very agitated when the coal started arriving at our compound, and his crestfallen looks signaled profound unhappiness and dismay.

Not long after, he appeared before me one morning at breakfast and announced he was sorry to report that the coal I purchased was no good. Most of it simply would not burn, he said, and many of the lumps were really rocks colored black. I had been badly cheated, he added, but he, Pien, might be able to help me out. If I would give him a free hand, Pien would get rid of the old coal and replace it with good coal that would burn. There would be some modest cost to bring about this switch, but Pien assured me it would be well worth it.

Recognizing that a household crisis of "face" was at hand, from which I had little chance of emerging the winner, I reluctantly agreed. Bypassing Pien as the intermediary in the first place had caused him great embarrassment, not to mention the loss of "squeeze" that servants expected to get on household purchases. He was now proposing a way to set this all straight. Accordingly, men appeared one day and appeared to be moving the old coal from the store room in the compound and replacing it with new coal. Pien was very much on hand, supervising the whole operation and checking from time to time that no strings were attached to the scales to give false weight. He would also ostentatiously inspect individual pieces of coal to make sure they were the genuine article. Once the transaction was completed he announced that everything was again satisfactory, and we would be happy to see how well this new coal would work.

Lyn and I both felt in advance the coal would not really change, that the whole charade was necessary to restore Pien's self esteem. Lyn demonstrated this to our satisfaction, though, by placing a small leaf upright between a couple of pieces of coal in our original pile. We both were gone during the day, when the replacement was supposed to be taking place, but when Lyn returned in the evening she found the small leaf still in its place in the coal pile. The coal was still the same, but now it burned brightly and easily.

A similar sort of incident occurred with the purchase of an electric iron. The one Pien had been using gave out, and Lyn unthinkingly bought a replacement in the Tung An market. Pien again protested that the new iron would not work properly, and Lyn allowed him to take it back and buy one of his own choice. This ended the discussion, and after that everything seemed to be working well. One day, sometime later, Lyn happened to be in the kitchen and noticed that Pien was ironing with a traditional Chinese iron, the kind that used live coals for heat instead of electricity. Because the iron Pien bought did not last long, and he was too embarrassed to report it or admit he had chosen poorly, he simply shifted to the old method of ironing. He never did ask for money to buy another electric iron, though these must still have been available in the local market, and we did not urge him to get one.

Most of those planning to leave North China had done so by the latter part of November. About sixty percent of the Americans in North China were in this category, including a large number of the people we knew well. The State Department language school people remained, as did some of the Fulbright scholars, some of the missionary board leaders, and a few others plus the ECA and

A China Story: From Peip'ing to Beijing

Consulate General staffs. For the most part, though, our social life declined quite drastically.

The people planning to stay in Peip'ing were now beginning to think about getting ready for a period of fighting, and the shortages that would come with a siege. We bought some bags of flour on the open market, as well as candles, kerosene, and a few canned goods of the staple variety. The U.S. government sent in a plane load of supplies for use by its official community in Peip'ing, and as members of that community ECA staff were permitted to buy from a commissary hastily set up to sell the supplies on the Consulate General's grounds. Since we had already put together a small emergency cache of things bought from the normal channels, we did not get around to visiting the commissary until a couple of days after it was declared open. This government shipment was an emergency supply for everyone's use, to be available if the city markets no longer functioned to supply our needs. Moreover, we assumed everyone would think the same way and use it sparingly. To our surprise, and disgust, we found almost everything in the store snapped up by the first people to get there. No rationing system had been employed, and no limits set on how much each family might buy of any item, so fear and greed had taken over.

People we knew in the language school bought so much flour, which they stacked in bags that reached from the floor to the ceiling, they could not possibly use it in a year's time. Other items were similarly hoarded. Although we were all about to be in any future unpleasantness together, as compatriots and colleagues, a spirit of shared hardship and cooperation among the official community was nowhere to be seen. I should add that the other ECA people were as slow as we, and also found nothing but empty shelves.

To shore up any flagging spirits among those staying behind, there was a formal dance at the Peking Club later in the month, probably sponsored by one of the diplomatic missions, and we attended. What I remember most is Lyn, though seven months pregnant, still able to get into a pale blue formal dress she bought before we were married. She looked lovely in it, and I was very proud of her. Perhaps the apron-like sash she wore with it did the trick, or maybe it was due to the earlier bout with hepatitis, but whatever it was she looked smashing and amazingly trim for one so late in a pregnancy.

Thanksgiving was approaching, and nothing much was planned to celebrate it. On a whim we decided to drive out to the Summer Palace, some miles outside the city, for a last look. We now knew it was only a short time until the city would be isolated, and we were taking a chance in venturing so far. Nevertheless, I was able to borrow one of the ECA jeeps for the day (it was, after all, an American holiday), and we stopped at Shishkin's Dairy for lunch makings. Shishkin's was called a dairy but it was also a delicatessen sort of place, run by White Russian émigrés, and there we picked up some rye bread, cold meats and cheese to take with us.

The countryside in late November was now cold and bleak, and quiet because field work was ended for the year. Few people seemed out and about in the villages we passed through. Bundled in U.S. Army parkas we had picked up on the local market, we managed to stay fairly comfortable in the open jeep despite wind and the low temperature.

When we reached our destination we found the entrance to the Summer Palace closed and the place deserted. Not wishing to give up on our idea without some effort to salvage a last look, we took a road that led along one side of the palace grounds. This eventually ran up a small rise and we found ourselves at a point where we could look down on, and to some degree down into, the Summer Palace. We parked the jeep, sat ourselves by the side of the road, and ate our Thanksgiving sandwich lunch while looking out on the view below. This was not the Summer Palace we knew, empty and drab in the gray autumn afternoon, but we sat and looked at it while sadly musing about what might happen to it, and whether we would ever see it again. Our lunch finished, we picked up the wrappings and headed back to the city. Hardly a traditional way to spend a Thanksgiving, as those things usually go, but for us it seemed to fit the mood of the place and time.

Shortly after Thanksgiving, Lyn and I were walking along Marco Polo Street in the Legation Quarter one afternoon, not going anywhere in particular but just getting a bit of exercise. Suddenly we heard sounds of commotion back on Legation Street. The papers had said there would a protest by students at the mayor's office over some government action, probably relating to housing conditions, and we assumed the noise we heard related to that protest. As we turned back to look at the intersection we saw trucks carrying mounted machine guns move up toward the crowd, and this was quickly followed by the sound of firing. Suddenly, people were running past us in the street in great confusion.

Not wanting to get caught in the fleeing mob we quickly ducked into the Peking Club, which we happened to be passing just at the time. There we waited until the street became quiet, then made our way home only after making certain the way was clear and the armed trucks had disappeared. This encounter was over in a short span of time, but the papers later reported that several students were injured and a few actually killed. The government was getting more and more nervous, opposition was becoming more visible, and the time for a final show-down was now very close.

CHAPTER THIRTEEN

"The ancient city of Peking is now being shelled by Communist guns! So says a San Francisco broadcast picked up here on shortwave today. I can imagine the excitement this is causing at home. Actually it is all nonsense. Firing, most of it southwest of the city, has been going on the greater part of the day, and around supper time became quite intense — enough to rattle our windows — while for the first time I hear the heavy booms clearly punctuated by the rat-tat-tat of machine guns. But so far as I know, no shots whatever have been directed into the city itself. Moreover, I suspect that ninety percent of the firing is the work of the Nationalist soldiers, who today are packing the city more than ever, and probably expend their ammunition so recklessly in the hope of scaring their enemies and encouraging themselves."

Derk Bodde, Peking Diary, Entry for December 15,1948, Henry Schuman, Inc., New York, 1950, p. 69.

Peip'ing, December/January 1948-49

Communist forces began to close in on Peip'ing December 13th, to the accompaniment of heavy artillery fire to the north and west of the city. In a matter of a few days the city's isolation was complete. The rail lines, roads and telephone wires were cut first; the power plant located outside the city at Shihchingshan was taken on December 15th, after which there was no power for light and no power to run the water pumps; the last remaining air field serving Peip'ing was abandoned on December 17th and taken over by the Communists the next day. Nationalist troops moved inside the city walls, for the most part in orderly fashion

151

and not in headlong retreat, for General Fu Tso Yi prepared to make his stand with those walls as protection. The front lines, the skirmish area, was quickly established at about one mile outside the city walls. An eight o'clock curfew went into effect inside the city, and no one appeared on the streets after that time except military patrols.

A last shipment of ECA flour reached Peip'ing from T'ientsin just before the railway line was cut, slightly more than 10,000 tons in large (100 pounds) and small (48 pounds) bags. Normally, supplies such as these would be received by the Peip'ing Ration Committee (which operated the program) and moved to their own storage facilities from whence the flour would be distributed to ration shops. This time, however, the routine was changed. My report of what happened, taken from ECA records, was as follows:

"... losses occurred when Nationalist troops, stationed near the Kuang An Men godown, began taking large amounts of flour for their own use, including one carload (1,360 bags) for which the then Governor of Hopei Province personally assumed the responsibility for replacing. Additional losses occurred when the military authorities loaned their vehicles to the Peip'ing Ration Committee to help move the flour to points of safety inside the city walls. During this movement, the soldiers doing the moving intimidated the civilian employees of the Ration Committee who were assigned the task of tallying the amounts moved, and took large quantities of flour for themselves. The military authorities stored the flour they did move in an open park near Ch'ien Men Gate, without permission from either ECA or the Ration Committee, and although police were assigned to guard the flour during the period it was stored in the open, further losses occurred at this point. It was not until the flour stored at Ch'ien Men was finally moved to the ECA compound and an accurate check taken, that our exact losses could be determined." In all, the troops took about 145 tons of flour, but 9,670 tons of this last shipment actually reached the ration shops.

One of the first activities undertaken by the defenders was to establish alternative landing strips inside the city, thus restoring some sort of air link with the south. Gangs of conscripted laborers were soon seen taking down the telephone and power poles and lines along the avenues that bordered the glacis around the Legation Quarter. This glacis, plus a large park area near the Temple of Heaven, were the only open spaces large enough, and flat enough, to accommodate landing aircraft, which is why they were chosen. The avenues along the glacis sported colorful ceremonial arches, called "p'ai lou," and these were also being dismantled to remove hazards to planes landing or taking off from the glacis. The damage caused by these activities was particularly sad in the case of the Temple of Heaven, where hundreds of lovely old trees were uprooted to make a landing strip that would have little real value in the defense of the city.

When these impediments were removed, a few fighter planes actually landed inside the city. Once down, though, they stayed there for several days. The ground of the glacis was soft, consisting of light, almost dusty soil, and planes could not get enough traction to build up speed for a takeoff. This was an embarrassing situation for the defenders, but some bright soul thought of a way around the problem.

The weather in Peip'ing was now quite cold, for winter had really arrived, and water was spread on the glacis to freeze the mud it created. This frozen surface provided enough traction to get the planes aloft. Even with operations restored, however, these makeshift air strips were never vital links with the outside world. The planes using them were mostly small fighters, and larger cargo or passenger aircraft rarely attempted to use the landing areas.

In addition to building landing strips, there was much activity in other parts of the city. Many poor people lived in shanty-type housing clustered outside the exterior walls of the city, and the military now moved to raze these houses to clear the area and improve the field of fire. This was the same military rationale that created the glacis around the Legation Quarter after the Boxer uprising at the turn of the century. Not only were thousands of men and boys rounded up to work on this clearance, but the people displaced from their homes now added to thousands of refugees seeking shelter from the cold weather. Other laborers were used to shore up the outer walls in places, carrying bricks and mortar for the purpose. Sometimes it was possible for a man to buy his way out of the labor conscription, but it was more common that the person selected had to spend a few days at this work and away from his usual job. Our Pien tried to get out of it, but was not successful, and neither was his helper, Ho.

Fighting during this time, and in fact throughout the forty days the city was under siege, never seemed very serious. During the day, and sometimes at night, one could hear the sounds of artillery and some small arms fire, but this seemed limited to the skirmish areas and rather far away. An occasional shell would be lobbed into the city, particularly at times when an airplane was landing or taking off from one of the air strips, but little damage was ever reported and little damage was visible as one moved about in the city. The ECA office was adjacent to the glacis landing strip, and just inside the walls of the Legation Quarter, and at times an exploding shell would sound very close. The danger from this was never considered serious enough to close down the office, though, or to move people to some sort of bomb shelter until the shelling died down.

More dangerous than the bombs was the food airlift. In what was probably more of a public relations effort than a genuine attempt to provide food, the government sent several planeloads of food (bags of flour and rice) over the city. Because the planes were too large to use the small landing areas newly created, they made no attempt to land. Instead, they circled the city and men simply pushed bags of food through the open doors of the planes to fall haphazardly onto the ground below. This proved neither accurate nor effective. Food was falling all over the city, causing scrambles among those close enough to get their hands on some of it, in some cases going through the roofs of houses, and even hitting an occasional unwary pedestrian or bicycle rider in the street. The impact of hitting the ground broke the bags, adding to the confusion and loss.

After of couple of such clearly unsatisfactory delivery attempts, the winter weather again inspired an alternative solution. This time the planes circled over some of the frozen lakes inside the city, dropping the food bags on the ice instead of onto the streets or over residential neighborhoods. While the lakes were indeed frozen, the ice was not thick enough to take the weight of falling hundred pound sacks, and food crashed through the ice to be lost in the water below. With this, no further attempts to supply food by air lift were made.

Our own food situation was never very precarious, although it did get a bit monotonous. Almost throughout the siege, carts carrying winter vegetables (cabbage, turnips and the like) were coming through the lines into the city, and some chicken and pork was usually available in the market. These items were costly, but not for us. The ECA office had been supplied with US$ funds in an amount considered ample to pay salaries and allowances for both American and local employees for an extended period of isolation. We therefore had access to US$, and prices in US$ stayed pretty much the same. Prices in GY$ deteriorated drastically, however, and those who depended on Chinese currency alone suffered severely.

In addition to fresh food, the markets had large stocks of canned goods, left over from military stores that had come with U.S. troops stationed in Peip'ing at the end of the war. Some of it probably came from stores turned over to Nationalist army units, and which they then sold on the open market. These canned items were mostly butter, cheese, powdered milk, and fruit juices, none of which were very much in favor with Chinese households. As a result, some of these canned goods were always available at quite reasonable prices, and to us they were most welcome.

We filled our bathtub with water at the first news hostilities had begun, and used this for cooking and limited washing purposes because water from the tap stopped running. But water mysteriously started running from time to time, and when it did we replenished our bathtub supply. Many houses in Peip'ing had their own wells, and were never in any trouble. This included houses and apartments in the American Consulate General's compound and most missionary compounds. For all these reasons, we never felt threatened by a lack of water.

In addition to the nearly ten thousand tons of flour that managed to get to the ration shops, ECA used a small part of the final shipment from T'ientsin to help other groups. About eight tons of flour were given to staff of the Peip'ing Ration Committee for their personal use, and 125 tons were given to various charitable groups such as hospitals, orphanages and schools. When these last distributions were completed, the small mountains of flour bags that had been piled near Ch'ien Men disappeared, and a more manageable amount, about 188 tons, was moved into the warehouse space in the ECA compound. Contrary to our own fortunate situation, and the contribution these final deliveries made to the wellbeing of some city residents, a large number of people among the poor and refugee groups had difficulty getting enough to eat, and suffered cruelly in the winter conditions. By some accounts, this figure reached as high as thirty percent of the people living in Peip'ing at the time.

As the siege continued, it became ever more evident that a takeover was imminent and there was no chance to escape from it. Foreigners such as we were not only concerned for the future of Chinese we knew personally, but were also intensely curious how these people viewed what lay in store for them. The response was pretty much the same among educated, professional people who had no strong Communist ties or leanings, and a couple of examples illustrate how thinking ran among this group.

One was an administrator of a city hospital, one of those selected to receive flour from the remaining ECA stocks. I had been with him arranging the delivery details, and when we finished our business we stepped outside onto a verandah on a top floor of the hospital, one which had a good view of the city stretched out below. As we surveyed the city from this vantage point I asked him what he thought would happen to people down there when the Communists took power. His reply was that he had no idea, but in his view it could not be much worse than the past had been.

He noted that the decline of the Empire under the Manchu dynasty, and the foreign acquisition of concessions in the Treaty Ports with their special privileges of all kinds, engendered popular dissatisfaction that led to the collapse of the Empire and the rise of a Chinese Republic. There was great hope for a while, but in short order China fell into an era of anarchy as rival war lords vied for power to exploit the areas they controlled. The Kuomintang Nationalist revolution of the late 1920s again brought a surge of hope that conditions might improve. But, before this new regime could consolidate its position, the Japanese attacked. For over a decade China was wracked by its struggle to survive as a nation, half or more of its territory under direct foreign control. Now come the Communists, brushing away yet another corrupt regime in which people had lost faith. In this man's view, what lay ahead was simply another step in what had been a protracted history of violent change and continuing disappointment for the Chinese. In sum, he said, who knows what will happen next? It may even be a little bit better, because it certainly cannot be much worse than what the Chinese had suffered over the previous fifty years.

Another version, this time by Dr. Khati Lim, took the view that she was Chinese, the Chinese had been around for a long time, and had survived harsh times often before in their history. She did not know whether the Communists would be good or bad, but this was her country, and she was not going to run away. If the Communists said take two steps forward and one step backward she, Dr. Lim, would do it. She had worked hard to acquire the medical skills she possessed, the Chinese would continue to have babies, and her country needed those skills. She proposed to offer them on any terms the new regime was prepared to use them. This was a gutsy, feisty attitude; together with the views of the hospital administrator they hardly amounted to jubilant expectations about life under the Communists.

Attitudes like these were hard for Americans back in the U.S. to under-stand — the pervasive feeling among intelligent people that amounted to calm, even stoic, acceptance of what would come. They had enough of war, political polarization, suffering and frustration; they were ready for the next act to begin, whatever it might be.

As the month wore on, foreigners still staying in the universities outside Peip'ing found they could make their way through the lines to visit friends inside the city walls. On several occasions we talked with people who had made this trip, and the process sounded remarkably casual. As the foreigners left the Communist lines and headed for the city, Communist pickets would point out where the Nationalist outposts were located and advise them to be careful. On approaching the Nationalist lines the foreigners would call out announcing who they were. Once recognized they were allowed through the lines and on into the city.

The return, usually the next day and in broad daylight, was a repeat of the trip in, though this time it was the Nationalist troops who pointed out the Communist lines and advised the foreigners to be careful. As they neared the Communist sentries they would be waved through. Sometimes a Communist guard would greet them by holding up his rifle and saying, "Meikuo tso te. Ting hao!" ["This is American-made. It is very good!"] The large amounts of mili-tary equipment captured in Manchuria were now being brought to bear on the Nationalist defenders of Peip'ing.

Christmas that year was not a noticeably merry time. The stores had little to offer, no Christmas trees were being brought through the Communist lines, obviously, and there was no electricity for lights even if you had a tree. The cur-few in effect meant that evening parties were out, and so we planned to spend a quiet Christmas Eve at home. I did not know what to get for Lyn. This was not because she had everything, but because things she might need and want were simply not available. Nevertheless, I wandered through the large Tung An market on Morrison Street, hoping some inspiration might strike me, and it did.

One of the stalls in the market had a little carved wooden statue of Kuan Yin, Goddess of Mercy. This was lacquered in gold, had a small lotus stand to hold it, and the knees of the seated goddess were brown, not gold, as though worn from repeated rubbing by some prior owner(s). I could not tell where this little statue came from, when it was made, or whether it was particularly valuable, but it was a delicate piece and I liked it immediately. I wandered away to look at other things, then returned and asked the price, wandered away again, asked the price again, and finally the seller and I struck a bargain.

To accompany this gift, I found a small leather-bound traveling case for toiletries in another stall, something Lyn could use some day whenever we were free to leave Peip'ing again. After we had finished our Christmas Eve dinner, and were seated by our coal stove in the living room, I gave Lyn my two gifts. These were not lavish, and the setting was certainly not the colorful, noisy Christmas we had the previous year in Canton. Many would say it was even a pretty dismal sort of time, but it was our first Christmas as a married couple that made it special, even if the gifts, decorations and festivities did not.

The next day, Christmas, we went to the American Consulate General's compound for a midday dinner with some of the language school families, Harriet Mills (a Fulbright scholar who opted to remain in Peip'ing) and Doak Barnett, a recently arrived correspondent. This was a chance to swap stories about what seemed to be happening from various vantage points, and get some sense of when and how the military situation might change. Doak was a particularly good source of information because it was his job to dig up what news he could, and this took him to places, and in contact with people, not available to the rest of us. Aside from some interesting gossip and a few anecdotes, however, we did not learn much that was new. But there was a sense, shared by most of us there, the situation was probably as bad as it would get, and this was comfort of a sort.

Social life did continue during the siege, if somewhat haphazard and low key for the most part. The head of the language school and his wife, the Sollenbergers, hosted parties for the American community from time to time. There were games to play (Bridge, Monopoly, Checkers), dancing, craft work for those so inclined, and a chance to be together in a large group. Evening dinner parties posed difficulties because of the food situation and the curfew, but daytime tea parties were back. Mostly, though, it was a quiet period socially compared to what it had been, but that was a far more active social life than most of us had ever known.

The streets during the day were crowded with people — soldiers, refugees, labor conscripts moving to their work sites, others going about their daily business. Soldiers were billeted everywhere, in parks, public buildings, abandoned houses, anywhere that had spare space. They were generally well behaved, but people did not want to cross them and tried to stay out of their way.

One evening Lyn and I were heading home up Morrison Street in an ECA jeep with its driver. Snow was falling lightly, and the street was crowded. A group of wounded soldiers was standing in the middle of the street, some with casts on arms or legs, some with crutches, and all dressed in padded winter greatcoats. They wanted a ride to wherever they were staying, and flagged down our car to get a lift, though there were far more of them than would fit into the jeep.

Once the car stopped they simply started to crowd in, neither noticing nor caring that Lyn and I were already in the back seat. As they jammed in, with their crutches, casts and bulky outer garments, we were quickly overwhelmed and not a little alarmed. Lyn, then eight months pregnant, cried out lest one of these hefty hitchhikers sit on her. She pointed to her stomach and said in her effective, if inelegant, Chinese, "Wo you hsiao hai tse li tou," roughly, ["I have a small child inside."] The soldiers looked at her in some stupefaction, as much for the fact that she said anything at all as for what she was saying, and for a moment it stopped the piling into the car. This gave us an opportunity to get out and tell the driver to take the soldiers where they wanted to go, after which he could return to the office. We walked the rest of the way to our compound, glad the incident ended so easily.

New Year's Eve was far different from the elegant time we spent in Hong Kong the year before. Neither of us can recall doing anything special to celebrate, so probably we spent the evening quietly together. We probably made some assessment of our situation, wondering what would happen next, and asking ourselves whether we had been foolish to stay in Peip'ing. The pregnancy was going well, as far as one could tell, but none of the baby things Lyn asked her mother to send had reached Peip'ing. These items would certainly not arrive now, so we had to find some way to better prepare for the baby's arrival. It is doubtful we spent a gloomy evening, because we never reached a point where we felt anything like fear or despair. On the other hand, the circumstances did not generate a buoyant, happy time either, one filled with the usual giddy, optimistic expectations the celebration of a New Year normally brings. Thinking back on it, New Year's Eve was probably just another night spent at home.

Last shipment of flour to reach Peip'ing before Communists cut the rail line, early December 1948

Jim at the flour "mountain" outside the train station

Flour ration line in Peip'ing in December 1948

Handing out flour at ration shop in Peip'ing, December 1948

CHAPTER FOURTEEN

"COMMUNISTS WIN ALL OF TIENTSIN; U.S. CITIZENS SAFE. BROADCAST REPORTS CAPTURE OF GARRISON CHIEF — PEIPING IS HELD NEXT TARGET"

New York Times, January 16, 1949, p. 1

"PEIPING SURRENDERS TO REDS AS NANKING REGIME OFFERS TO CONFER ON FOE'S TERMS; WAR IN NORTH ENDS; TRANSITIONAL COALITION IS ARRANGED — SAFETY ASSURED FOREIGNERS"

New York Times, January 23, 1949, p. 1

Peip'ing, January 1949

To most foreigners in Peip'ing, the battle for the city had many comic opera aspects. There seemed few casualties from the fighting, and there was no serious effort to level the city by shelling; the Nationalists seemed ready to settle down behind the walls for an indefinite period, and the Communists seemed in no hurry to force them out. Rumors persisted that negotiations of some kind were under way to settle the fighting, without damage to Peip'ing, and these were given credence by the sight one day of streetcars running. Electric power was being allowed into the city for limited uses, and this was one of them. Houses were still without lights, but people were again riding back and forth to work. The water supply also returned in the same mysterious fashion, and the work of dismantling the p'ai lou suddenly stopped. Some attributed this latter development to an ancient curse that decreed severe punishment for anyone who damaged a p'ai lou, but cynics saw it only as further evidence of a deal in the making. Passage of people and goods back and forth through the lines had been possible almost from the start of the siege. Taking all these things into consideration, the overall impression was this was not a serious battle in progress, only a make-believe one. The poor and homeless certainly had a hard time through it all, but as time passed it seemed less and less likely that severe fighting or heavy bombardment would ever take place.

General Fu Tso Yi did begin negotiations with the Communists in early January. Any bargaining power he once may have had disappeared with the surrender of many of his personal troops in other parts of North China, and the capture of T'ientsin on January 15th after severe fighting. That was the final push needed for settlement, and Fu Tso Yi's headquarters announced a truce on January 22nd. Occupation of the city by the Communists was scheduled for February 1st, which left the Nationalists nominally in charge of maintaining internal order during the intervening period.

The truce brought an end to one kind of uncertainty, but a new one quickly took its place. People felt relief that fighting with the Communists was at an end, but now there was unease about how the defeated, though still armed, Nationalist soldiers might behave. Chinese feared there might be one final round of looting and pillaging before the soldiers were finally forced to leave the city. The foreigners had a different worry. One rumor, unfortunately quite credible, said that pro-Nationalists (not specified as to whether they would be soldiers or Kuomintang Party activists) would attack foreigners just as the Communists were starting to enter the city. The ensuing massacre would therefore look like the work of the Communists, and publicity about this outrage could be used to draw foreign support to the waning Nationalist fortunes.

A PAS student of Lyn's, who lived close to us in the Nai Tse Fu area, appeared at the door one day to bring this rumor to our attention and offer his assistance if we were bothered in any way. We had heard the same rumor, and were concerned about it, but somehow the idea that a sixteen-year-old stripling could save us from a murderous attack actually seemed funny. We had the option to move into the American Consulate General's compound if we wished, but it seemed safer to stay in our isolated house in a Chinese residential area than to be in a place full of other Americans. And so we waited out a tense week, made doubly so by the imminent arrival of the baby.

Peip'ing, January 28, 1949

Starting about the time of the truce announcement, Ritchie Davis ordered an ECA driver and jeep to stay at our house each night until the baby was born. The city was still under curfew, no taxis or other transportation were about, and without a car at the door there would be no way to get Lyn to the hospital. Sometime after midnight, the morning of January 28th, Lyn woke me and said she thought it was time to leave for the hospital. The contractions, which we timed as carefully as we could, were coming at alarmingly close intervals, and the bag of waters had burst. The time had come, and after dressing warmly we set out for PUMC in the jeep.

The night was quite cold, and the streets deserted because of the curfew. The ride to the hospital was not far, and as we approached the major intersection of Morrison Street and Teng Shih K'ou, an armed soldier stepped forward to stop us, brandishing his rifle as he did so. The driver explained our reason for being out at the hour, in violation of the curfew, and the soldier looked into the car to see if this explanation made sense. After a short pause he waved us through, and in a few minutes we arrived at the hospital entrance.

The door was opened by an elderly Chinese woman who was either a charwoman or an amah, not one of the professional staff. She allowed us to enter and asked why we had come. I tried to explain that my wife was expecting a baby, to which she asked, in Chinese, "Is it number one?" This did not make much sense to me at first, and we went back and forth a bit with my explanation and her question. Finally it dawned on me that she was asking if this were the first child, and at that point I replied "yes," it was number one. At this the old lady pointed to some nearby chairs and told us politely to "wait a bit," meanwhile going back to her own chair by the door. It soon became obvious, from her inaction, that she believed all first babies took a long time arriving and there was no hurry to notify anyone else. In some desperation I set off along the hospital corridor in search of someone who could help, and soon found a nurse who both spoke English and would come back with me to talk with Lyn. In short order the nurse established that things had progressed rather dramatically, told the old amah to waken the doctor, and took Lyn and me up to a waiting room adjacent to the delivery room.

At that point I was dismissed and advised to wait outside in the hall. The doctor and other nurses quickly materialized, and I was aware only of a considerable amount of bustle and commotion going on in the delivery area. After what must have been no more than about twenty minutes of pacing the hall, a nurse emerged and asked if I would like to see the birth. This was not something I had counted on doing, and to my knowledge watching your child's birth was not even allowed in American hospitals in those days. My interest was aroused by the invitation though, and not wanting to appear the stereotyped craven, frazzled, frightened father-to-be, I agreed.

The staff did not let me into the delivery room itself, but I stood at a door with a glass window located behind Lyn's head. I could not see all that went on from that vantage point, but it was as much as I was ready to see that morning. Dr. Khati Lim, the physician in charge, was such a tiny woman that a platform had been built all around the delivery table to allow her to move anywhere she needed to be, and at the correct height. I remember she had a quick, jaunty manner, a pair of bright brown eyes, and wore a pair of exquisite jade earrings that peeked out from under her surgical cap.

As I reached the door, the birth process was already well started. Lyn did not have any anesthetic because, largely at the insistence of Maggie Boorman, she had become a convert to the cause of "natural childbirth," a relatively new obstetrical option back in the U.S. at the time. When Lyn asked Dr. Lim, sometime during the early stages of pregnancy, whether she would cooperate in a birth without an anesthetic, the doctor had replied, "My dear, we Chinese have been bearing babies for thousands of years without anesthetics."

Lyn was perspiring freely, and from time to time giving a moan or low call. At one point Dr. Lim asked her to hold back for a moment while she attended to something, and then the baby was there. Dr. Lim held up a small, crying creature that appeared to be covered in a soapy lather, and I could not tell whether it was a boy or girl. Some further follow-up work absorbed the doctor's attention for a few minutes, but I could not see what it was. Finally, the birthing was over.

A China Story: From Peip'ing to Beijing

A baby girl lay swaddled in a basket in a corner, Lyn was relaxed and resting, and I was swamped in all kinds of emotions, among which relief and pride were probably uppermost.

Dr. Lim looked toward the door and said I could now enter if I wished. Turning to Lyn, she asked if there was anything she wanted. When Lyn said she wanted a cigarette, I came bustling through the door lighting two at the same time in imitation of a Humphrey Bogart movie. Dr. Lim's comment was not approving. In all her years of practice, she said, she had never known a new mother to ask for a cigarette on the delivery table. We were too pleased with ourselves to take the rebuke very seriously, and chatted happily together as the nurses made preparations to move Lyn to her room and the baby to the nursery.

The baby Nancy, for that was to be her name, was fair-haired, even-featured, and came with a lovely yellow cast to her skin, the result of Lyn's hepatitis early in the pregnancy. Nancy created something of a stir when Chinese came to visit the nursery because they found it hilarious to see a blond-haired, yellow-skinned foreign baby among the dark-haired Chinese children. Nancy had also been born on the last day of the Lunar Year. The day after her birth, the 29th, was the first day of the new Year of the Ox. In Chinese tradition, a child is one year old on the day he or she is born; at the turn of the Lunar New Year the child becomes a year older. Thus, Nancy was two years old the day after she was born.

When I got back to the house, Pien was anxiously waiting for news of the birth, and he got right to the heart of matters when he asked, "Is it a baby, or is it a girl?" Clearly, girls did not count as babies, and when I assured him that we really did have a baby girl he managed to mask his disappointment somewhat, smiled and said, "Well, you'll certainly have a baby next time!"

The Chinese New Year was widely celebrated in the city, although somewhat less boisterously and lavishly than in previous times. Everyone was waiting expectantly for the first Communists to enter the city, which they did beginning January 31st with some advance parties. The grand entry parade was scheduled for February 3rd. ECA had been informed by Consulate radio, meanwhile, that a plane might be sent to evacuate the American staff before the Communist takeover became complete. We were therefore ordered to have ourselves ready to leave on short notice in the event arrangements for a safe landing and takeoff could be made.

Two days after Nancy was born, Lyn left the hospital and was driven home to pack and await further word about the evacuation flight. Nancy stayed in the hospital, and Lyn returned there periodically to nurse her. We were told to prepare no more than one bag per adult, including whatever we would be taking for the baby. It was amazing how easily we could decide what were the bare necessities. With Lyn supervising from a living room chair, we quickly packed our bags — a couple of changes of clothing for each of us adults, some toilet goods, and a fair amount of space devoted to diapers, shirts, blankets and similar baby things. No room for wedding presents, souvenirs, or anything heavy or bulky.

We had not been able to accumulate much in the way of baby equipment to start with, but a few weeks earlier we had found an American woman, wife of a free-lance writer, who was willing to sell us some used diapers and baby clothing. They were in appalling condition, and should have been given away, but we bought them for US $70 and were glad to have even that much. The diapers were in such poor condition it took two full washings to rid them of the stench of urine; the little shirts and outer garments were stained and full of holes. Whatever their condition, they were vital goods and received priority in the packing. We also bought a wicker basket, complete with handles, and fitted it with padded siding and a little padded mattress. This was to serve as her crib when she came home from the hospital, but would equally serve to carry her with us wherever, whenever, and however we might travel.

We waited throughout the day of the 31st, and finally toward evening learned that plans for the evacuation flight had been cancelled. Reasons were never given, but it was probably because sufficient guarantees of safe conduct could not be obtained from both the Nationalists and the Communists. At that point I took Lyn back to the hospital where she again fell into the post-natal routine that had been so precipitately interrupted. My feelings were mixed. On the one hand, I was glad to have them back under excellent care again; on the other, we were still in Peip'ing, facing an uncertain situation and an indefinite wait ahead.

Passport photo of Lyn, with Nancy,
age 10 weeks

Nancy standing in front of the
PUMC Hospital where she was born

CHAPTER FIFTEEN

> *"...I have seen no trace of discrimination against individual private foreigners other than that, for travel outside the city, they must have special passes — apparently not readily obtainable. On the official level, however, the situation is different. On the grounds that no diplomatic relations exist between themselves and the rest of the world, the Communists resolutely deny that the foreign consulates have any legal existence. In Tientsin they have confiscated the stocks of E.C.A. flour, thus bringing the activities of this organization in North China to an end."*
>
> Derk Bodde. Peking Diary [Entry for February 13, 1949], Henry Schuman, Inc., New York, 1950, p. 109.

Peip'ing, February 1949

On the day of the big parade, February 3rd, I visited with Lyn at the hospital for a while and then left to see what I could. The parade route moved through the northwest part of the city, entering by the Hsi Chih Men gate. I found a place to stand in a crowd along one of the avenues, and watched as troops, trucks and other vehicles moved past in impressive numbers and order. The trucks, weapons and equipment generally seemed to be American, mostly captured in the earlier battles for Manchuria. Some Japanese equipment must have been included, as well as military gear from a variety of other sources, but the bulk of it looked American.

From time to time a truck would pass by filled with young people, civilians by their dress, waving flags and banners and shouting slogans. They were acting as cheerleaders, inviting the people to respond by waving back and shouting, and close behind them came a truck with movie cameras aboard. The object was to get pictures of happy people welcoming the liberating army, and in that they must have been successful because people were responding. Once trucks of this kind had gone by, however, the crowd quieted down and watched the parading troops without much waving and shouting. They were not a hostile crowd; they just stood quietly at the roadside, showing few feelings of any kind.

After about an hour of watching I turned away and went back to the office. The Communist troops were certainly a well-equipped, well-disciplined lot, exuding an aura of confidence and high purpose as they marched by. Just by looking at them one could see why they had prevailed over the ragtag, nondescript soldiers who made up much of the Nationalist forces seen around the streets of Peip'ing. There seemed to be no sense of humiliation among defeated National troops in the part of the city where I was standing. My overall impression was the change in regimes taking place as I watched did so in an atmosphere that was strangely uncharged, lacking in bitterness at losing, lacking in joy at the prospect of a new leadership, but with much pageantry and, yes, a certain dignity.

There was little in our daily routine to indicate that new authorities were in charge. The ECA office remained open, though there was little to do, the hospital functioned as usual, the markets were again operating normally, and people seemed to be coming and going about their business as they always had. The immediate pressure of the siege was gone, but the air of expectancy was a bit like waiting for the proverbial second shoe to drop. My first direct contact with a Communist came a few days after the entry parade.

I had been visiting Lyn and Nancy in the hospital one afternoon, and when I returned to the waiting jeep I was alarmed to see a Communist officer having a lively argument with the driver. In fact, the officer was waving his arms and brandishing a pistol at the driver. When I reached the car the driver quickly told me the officer had asked to see a driver's permit. When the one produced proved to be issued by the previous city government, the officer declared the car illegally on the street and he would have to impound the car and jail the driver. I then asked the officer, in my far from fluent Chinese, to explain what the problem was, and managed to get more or less the same story from him.

My first gambit was to coax the officer to relax and let us take the car back to the ECA compound. We would promise not to drive it again until car and driver were properly licensed. This did not get far at all, so I then argued that before doing anything drastic he should talk with Ritchie Davis. I further explained that Mr. Davis had been born in China, spoke good Chinese, and would be happy to do whatever was necessary to ensure that the car was properly registered with the new authorities. To my surprise, the officer agreed, probably because he had never had dealings with foreigners before and was enjoying this opportunity to see what they were like at first hand. On our way to Ritchie's house, which we walked rather than driving in the car, the officer and I fell into conversation. Part of it, again in Chinese, went something like this:

Officer: "How long have you been in China?"

Hendry: "Nearly two years."

Officer: "You certainly don't speak very good Chinese if you've lived here that long."

Hendry: "That's true, but a large part of the time I was living in Canton, and they don't speak very good Mandarin there, either. Do you speak Cantonese?"

Officer: "No. That city is very far away."

Fortunately, Ritchie was at home when we arrived, and after my initial explanation of why we had come he entered into spirited discussion with the officer. I think the officer was very impressed with Ritchie's language skill, and maybe a little overawed by the surroundings, for he eventually agreed to let the driver return the jeep to the ECA compound. There it would stay until Ritchie had done whatever was necessary to get a permit of some kind. This was bound to be a sticky matter because ECA was an agency of the U.S. government, which did not recognize the new Communist regime, and the Communists did not recognize the U.S. What kind of permit would cover such a situation, and who would issue it, could involve a great deal of haggling. Nevertheless, for the moment the agreement reached by Ritchie and the officer was enough keep the driver out of jail and get the jeep back into the compound.

Lyn and Nancy returned home from the hospital on February 6th. A few days before that Maggie Boorman had given birth to a son, pretty much on the schedule all of us had calculated. Ten days was then the normal post-natal stay in a hospital, and when it was time to leave the nurses insisted that Lyn go to the exit door in a wheel chair. This was another part of the standard hospital procedure, but it seemed a little silly because a week earlier Lyn had walked out of the hospital on her own to get ready for possible evacuation. No amount of argument could convince the nurses that a wheel chair was unnecessary, and that is the way we left PUMC — Lyn in a wheel chair, I carrying Nancy, and a hospital servant carrying a suitcase with Lyn's and Nancy's effects.

The PUMC hospital, being a public institution, was required to keep its accounts in GY$, but the inflation had raged so violently, and so rapidly, there was no way periodic increases in fees and charges, or any normal billing process, could keep up with it. When I checked Lyn and Nancy out of the hospital I promptly paid the bill, but even so the cost of the delivery, doctor's fee, a private room and ten days of care for mother and baby amounted to about US$35. To put this in some perspective, one observer (Derk Bodde) estimated that the price of flour in Peip'ing had increased 4,500 times over the year that was ending just as Nancy was born.

Once settled back home Nancy, in her basket, was placed on the camphor chest at one side of our bed. There was not space for anything more elaborate in that small bedroom, but it was adequate for the time being. People kept dropping by to see the new baby, and between nursing Nancy and greeting visitors Lyn had reasonably full days. One day, shortly after the return, Mary Ferguson and Helen Beaumont appeared bearing a welcoming shaker of martinis. Beth Shaw also happened to stop by at the same time, and found Lyn holding court with a martini glass at her elbow, a cigarette in hand, and nursing Nancy. This jolted Mrs. Shaw's missionary values considerably, though she had great affection for Lyn, and with a pained look she protested, "Oh Lyn, not while you're nursing the baby!"

We decided against having an amah to look after Nancy, which left us unable to go out in the evenings unless we took the baby along with us. There were not many opportunities to do this, though, and we tended to stay pretty close to home. Daytime visits became the bulk of our social life, and in the evenings we sat together by the stove talking over all that was happening around us.

At some point during this period, I awakened one night feeling ill and made for the bathroom, where I passed out and fell to the floor. Lyn heard the thump, got up to see what had happened, and when she failed to rouse me called loudly for Pien to come and help her. Pien sized up the situation instantly, quickly dragged me from the bathroom, put me on the bed, and opened every window and door in the house to the freezing weather outside. He had recognized my state as an attack of coal gas poisoning, a common occurrence in North China. Coal was the main fuel in winter, and leaky stoves in closed surroundings caused many deaths. Pien's next move was to waken Nancy, make sure she was crying and therefore inhaling the cold fresh air, then cover her warmly in her basket. By this time the brisk air had begun to revive me, and Pien insisted that I walk around the court yard as rapidly as possible. He also put out the fire in the sitting room stove.

All this had taken about half an hour, and it was still only three or four in the morning. We huddled in our coats, or walked around, killing time until we could make our way to a safer place. About seven in the morning we took off for the American Board mission compound, where the Shaws lived. The Shaws' house was centrally heated, so they had no coal gas problems, and they took us in as though we were their own children. That was pretty much the way we felt, too, as safe and again comfortable we settled down at the Shaws' place for the day.

Pien quickly arranged for someone to inspect the sitting room stove and make the necessary repairs. The repair man found a small hole, the diameter of a pin, in the stove pipe, and this was the source of the gas leak. As Lyn and I reconstructed things, the chair where I usually sat in the evenings was low to the ground, and the coal gas accumulated near it at floor level. Over a period of time I absorbed enough coal gas into my system to bring on the collapse. Lyn tended to sit on the sofa, which she preferred because it was a higher, more comfortable, place to nurse Nancy. For that reason both Lyn and Nancy were less exposed than I had been. Thanks to Pien's prompt action in getting the windows open, my bad effects from the incident were limited to a headache for the rest of the day. The faulty stove pipe was replaced and we moved back into the house the same night.

The Communists continued to keep a fairly low profile in the early days, and only on one occasion did officials of some kind come to the house. Three or four of them, one being a woman, knocked at the front gate and said they wanted to inspect the house. After looking around in a cursory way, not really searching seriously for anything, they asked if we had a radio transmitter. We replied we did not, and in fact did not even have a radio of any kind. The next question was whether we had guns or ammunition, and again we answered in the negative. That seemed to satisfy them and they left, and that was the only time we were ever searched or questioned while we remained in Peip'ing.

The ECA compound got off less easily, however. The account I wrote for ECA included the following picture:

"On February 18, 1949, officials representing the Communist Military Control Commission appeared at the ECA compound where the balance of undistributed flour was stored. After forcing the Regional Director to draw the bolt on the godown door, they removed all ECA flour stored in the compound. ECA received no written statement showing the amount taken, and was not informed as to the destination or ultimate distribution of the flour and, since the Communists refused to recognize the existence of ECA, it was impossible to prevent or modify the confiscation in any way. The amount taken totaled 187.85 L.T., and is carried in the accounts as taken by Communist authorities."

With the removal of the flour, any rationale for keeping the ECA office open also disappeared. There was literally no basis to continue any of the programs, and therefore no recourse but to close up shop and leave as soon as possible. What followed was a period, fortunately not very long, of confusion and deadlock. The Communists would not let ECA operate, but they would not let the staff go; staff who applied for exit visas were told these could not be issued because the ECA and/or the U.S. government were not recognized by the new regime. At this same time, the British government recognized the new regime, an action reciprocated by the Communists. When we learned exit visas would be issued if we could get passage on a ship departing from T'ientsin, the British shipping company, Jardine Matheson, told us they would book passage only for those who held exit visas. And there things sat for a while. Foreigners were free to move about in the city but, Americans in particular, could not leave the city.

Not knowing when the situation would change was irksome, but no one felt particularly threatened by it. The Communists had been quite proper in their treatment of people, and although they were now obviously in charge of things they tended to stay in the background. Mostly, it was a period of boredom. Nothing much to do, subdued social life, and little contact with the outside world. Finally, early in March, word came to the ECA office that exit visas would be granted to any staff who applied for them. This was the word we had been awaiting, and now began to make departure plans. We would be among the first group of foreigners to leave Peip'ing after its capture and among the second group of foreigners to leave North China via T'ientsin.

A China Story: From Peip'ing to Beijing

At this point, since ECA would pay for the shipment of household effects, Lyn and I decided to make a modest investment in some Chinese furniture. We had long admired the furniture of North China, with its clean lines, lustrous brown woods (called "huang hua li," or "hua li"), and fine brass fittings. Our current house had some examples of this, chests and tables, as did the first house, and many other foreigners had acquired some of this handsome furniture. There was certainly no guarantee a household shipment would ever reach the States, since the national recognition stalemate seemed to preclude international shipments between China and the U.S. But Chinese merchants are a clever and imaginative group, and if a merchant agrees to a business obligation he usually takes great pains to make good on it. The furniture seemed worth the gamble.

The furniture merchants of Peip'ing were in a particularly vulnerable spot in early 1949. They did not know whether, or under what conditions, they would be allowed to continue their usual business. Their stock in trade was large and bulky, difficult to hide, unlike dealers in jewelry or precious metals. The choice the furniture shops faced was either to liquidate their inventories, for whatever hard currency they could get, or keep what they had and hope they could stay in business. Even if allowed to stay in business, however, the prospects were dim that either foreign tourists or wealthy Chinese would be coming to their stores very soon. The result was a buyer's market the likes of which one rarely finds in a lifetime.

We were in better financial shape a year after our marriage than ever expected. Plans for what to do when back to the States were still highly uncertain, but now there was a larger cushion of savings to see us through. Given the favorable change in circumstances, we decided to gamble with US $100; if we never saw the purchases again, the loss would be affordable. Rugs would be nice, as would art work or porcelain, but it was furniture we really wanted to take back from China. Venturing into the part of the Chinese City where furniture was sold, from one shop we selected a pair of large chests (probably dating from the early part of the nineteenth century), an altar table, and a coffee table; from a second shop we bought another altar table, classic in its lines and beautifully simple. After a small amount of haggling, not very serious in either shop, the total cost came to US $105, a tad more than our upper limit. The shops arranged for packing the purchases and eventually shipping them, and billed the American Consulate General for these costs. To jump ahead in the story, the furniture was delivered to us in the U.S., and only a few weeks after we ourselves had reached there.

One morning not long before we were due to leave Peip'ing, Lyn received a telephone call from one of the State Department wives, asking if she could come to visit and bring a couple of her friends. Lyn agreed and invited the group for tea that afternoon. After tea had been served, and a certain amount of social chit chat had taken place, one of the ladies asked what we proposed to do with supplies left over from the siege. She was referring, of course, to foodstuffs such as flour and canned goods that had come to Peip'ing in the emergency U.S. government supply shipment the previous November, at the time the last evacuation of foreigners took place.

Lyn replied we did not have any supplies because the commissary had been emptied by the time we first reached it. The ladies clearly did not believe this, and continued to ask to see our "supplies," with some emphasis. Lyn again said we had no stocks in the house, and added that they could help themselves to what we had. With that she opened the door to one of the Chinese chests in the sitting room. On the bottom shelf were three or four large cans of orange juice, a large can of cheese and a can of butter. Seeing this pitiful excuse for an emergency stockpile, the women apologized profusely for bothering Lyn, and departed in embarrassed haste. Beaming broadly, Lyn bade them goodbye; inwardly, she was enjoying the clear discomfort of people whose selfishness in the face of a common problem had so infuriated and saddened her.

Winter uniform with knapsacks

Driving pack mules in victory parade.

Communist troops driving American
vehicles, captured from the defeated
Nationalists

Photo credit for all three photos:

James Burke/Graphic House, appearing in *National Geographic*, Vol. XCVI, No.
3, September 1949, pages 338, 364, and 368.

CHAPTER SIXTEEN

Peip'ing, March 1949

The time to leave Peip'ing finally arrived. Although we had already packed to leave once before, back in January, this time we planned to take more than just clothing. There was some bedding and towels that would prove useful, Lyn's wedding gown, the presents we had received at our wedding, and a few other things picked up over the year. We managed to find a steamer trunk in the local market and filled it with these items. This would go as hold luggage as far as Hong Kong, and be shipped on to the States from there. The camphor chest went with the furniture just purchased. Otherwise, because porters were not available in a Communist society, we were told to take only one suitcase each. This we could manage on our own while also carrying Nancy between us in the wicker basket.

A few Americans were still planning to stay on, at least for as long as the Consulate General remained open, and many of these came by the house to say goodbye. We gave our faithful duo, Pien and Ho, a generous severance bonus, all the equipment we had bought for the house, and any stores of food and coal that remained. They had been loyal and helpful to us throughout the time we had known them, and I probably owed my life to Pien. We were sad to leave them, not knowing what they would find to do next. Many of the former PAS students came to wish us well, promising to stay in touch if possible and hoping to meet again some day in the States.

Exit visas were issued on March 17th, 1949, and were good for travel to Shanghai if used during the period March 17th to March 31st. The ship on which passage was booked was not stopping in Shanghai, but going directly from T'ientsin to Hong Kong. Additional visas were needed from the British Consulate in Peip'ing for transit through Hong Kong on the way to Shanghai. These were issued on March 18th, and with that our documentation for departure was complete.

After a final lunch at the house the next day, March 19th, we wrapped Nancy warmly in her little traveling basket, picked up the two suitcases, and headed for the train station. An American friend came with us, a Fulbright scholar who was staying on in order to finish her doctoral thesis. She saw to our tickets and generally made sure we were getting on the right train. Once assembled at the station, we made up a traveling party of eight — Ritchie Davis, another American ECA staff member who was accompanied by the foreign correspondent she had been living with, an Austrian refugee couple (he had been responsible for managing ECA's accounts), and our family of three.

Just as we were getting ready to leave, up ran one of Lyn's former students bearing a gift, actually two boxes. A rather emotional farewell scene followed, because this particular student had been something of a sycophant of Lyn's, but it was soon over and we turned to go. Filing through the gate to board our train, a Communist guard asked to inspect our exit visas. He seemed to be having some trouble making out the details, and in exasperation our American friend reached out and turned the document around in his hand. The young man, probably unable to read well to start with, was holding the visa upside down! For a moment I thought his embarrassment at being publicly corrected by our friend would anger him, and we would not be allowed to proceed, but he waved us through and we climbed on board the train for T'ientsin.

T'ientsin, March 1949

The trip to T'ientsin was uneventful. Nancy seemed to travel well, but attracted attention from Chinese passengers anxious to glimpse a foreign baby. Somewhere along the way Lyn decided to open the present she had just received. To her surprise, and with a certain amount of distaste, she discovered the gift consisted of two boxes of grilled small birds, complete with heads and feet. Ritchie told us this was a very special delicacy, expensive to buy, and clearly an honor to receive. Lyn was pleased with this news, but quickly closed the boxes and tucked them out of sight without offering them around the group. No one pressed her to do so.

By the time we arrived in T'ientsin it was dark and cold, and had started to rain. Guards on the platform ordered us to stand to one side while all the Chinese passengers moved into the station. When the platform was clear of everyone but our party, the guards ordered us to open our suitcases for inspection. This went without a hitch until they began to go through the contents of the two who had been living together. Their passports and visas were in their own names, since they were not married, but their clothing and other personal items were scattered indiscriminately through their two bags. This was a very suspicious matter for the guards, and there was a lengthy conversation about what to make of it. Higher authority was summoned from somewhere inside the station and, after asking some further questions through Ritchie as interpreter, the officer allowed us to proceed on our way.

The wait, which may have been a half hour to forty-five minutes in length, was enough to make us all thoroughly cold and damp. Nancy was beginning to cry because she was chilled and ready for some nourishment. Outside the station two cars were waiting for us, and once we had all climbed inside they quickly took us to our next destination, the apartment of the branch manager of the National City Bank of New York in T'ientsin. The manager was a brother-in-law of Ritchie's who, though away somewhere himself, had made arrangements for us to stay in his apartment until we left for Hong Kong two days later. As we entered this luxurious, not to say palatial, accommodation we were aware of suddenly passing from the bottom of the heap (huddled refugees on the dingy train platform) to the top, where warmth, comfort and light abounded.

Lyn, Nancy and I were given the manager's bedroom for our use, and that room alone was probably bigger than our house in Peip'ing. After freshening up from the trip and feeding Nancy, we joined the others for dinner. This was an event memorable because the first course consisted of small clams in the shell, prepared in a sauce of tomato, garlic and onion, and as tasty as anything I had ever eaten. When finished with the first offering, the man waiting on table offered a second helping. I quickly accepted the offer, and continued from there until finally putting away 40-50 of the little gems. Others, including Lyn, also took second helpings, but I recall out-eating everyone else by a substantial margin. I paid for this indulgence with indigestion during the night, but so did Nancy who must have ingested some of the clams' potent seasoning with her night feeding. To compliment the cook, we gave him the two boxes of grilled birds Lyn had received. He seemed very pleased and flattered at the gift.

Our brief stopover in T'ientsin was comfortable and pleasant in the City Bank apartment, but we were getting edgy about leaving. On the morning of March 21st we drove to the dockside for departure, and made our way to where boarding formalities and Customs inspections were to take place. The ship on which we would travel to Hong Kong was anchored at T'aku Bar, some 35 miles away at the mouth of the Hai River. Ships of the same size normally came up the river as far as T'ientsin, but none had been allowed to do so since the Communists had taken charge. To reach our ship, a tug and barge were standing ready to take us down the river, and a small crowd of both foreigners and Chinese was waiting to board.

Before this was allowed, all luggage had to be inspected. This included our suitcases and the trunk going into the ship's hold. The inspectors, a mixture of Customs officers and soldiers, examined first the wedding gifts and other items we had put into our trunk. The officers were looking for art treasures that foreigners or Chinese might be smuggling out of the country. We were very proud of some of our things, wedding presents in particular, and wondered if there would be any problem getting them cleared. We need not have worried; the Customs people quickly concluded our possessions were far from what interested them. "This stuff is just junk," said one of them to his colleagues as he shut the trunk and stamped it "cleared." We were not prepared to argue the point, but it was a devastating put-down.

Next came our hand luggage. We were not concerned with what they might find in it, because it held only clothing and personal effects, but Lyn had taken the precaution of wrapping our hoard of U.S. dollars in waxed paper and putting this in the fold of Nancy's diapers. The soldiers prodded around Nancy's basket, feeling under the mattress and even using the point of a bayonet to poke the mattress contents a bit. Finding nothing of interest, we were waved through that part of the inspection as well. Inwardly enormously relieved to be at this stage and undetected, we now began the wait for all the others to be examined.

This was a lengthy wait, too, and well after noontime before the Customs formalities were completed. As we started to board, the officer in charge announced that only Chinese would be permitted on the tugboat, which had a cabin; foreigners would make the trip on the open barge that was pulled behind. The barge had no toilet facilities, and no protection from the wind. North China is still cold in March, and the trip would take five to six hours, so we hunkered down on the deck and pulled up our parka hoods to get as much cover as we could. Nancy's basket had warm blankets, and the padded sides provided some wind protection, but we put a bit of material over the top, like a tent, to give added warmth.

The only other group to make this trip down the river earlier in the month had been fired upon from the banks, apparently because word had not reached some villages that Communist authorities approved the river travel. We all felt some apprehension on this account, naturally, and all eyed the banks warily as our small tug and barge caravan began its journey. Nothing happened, as it turned out. People did appear on the river banks at places and waved, but that was all. Although the countryside at that time of the year was much browner and bleaker than I remembered from my previous trip down the same river, the fact no one was firing at us made it beautiful.

No provision had been made to feed us on the trip, and we had neglected to bring food or water with us. Nancy got hungry, like the rest of us, but her food supply had not been left behind. When it was time for Lyn to start nursing, I became anxious this be done as discreetly as possible, a concern that Lyn found hilarious in our ridiculous circumstances. Chinese women, after all, nursed their babies openly all over the place; I was silly to be so upset about a perfectly normal function. Nevertheless, I stood in front of Lyn and Nancy with my parka open as a screen. Nobody seemed very interested in any of this, however, and I wound up looking and feeling pretty foolish.

At long last we came to the mouth of the river and could see the coastal steamer at anchor waiting for us. By this time the light was beginning to fail, and everyone was cold, tired and cranky. Nancy was no exception, but she could give voice to her discomfort and did so, fussing and crying intermittently. A large float served as a dock for boarding, from which passengers mounted a companionway on the ship's side to the main deck of the vessel. As the tug and barge came alongside the float we all climbed down onto it, but some made an immediate rush for the companionway.

The Communist officer in charge of the boarding stopped the rush with a shout, and announced that things were different now that the Revolution had triumphed. The boarding would be orderly, he said; women and children would go first, followed by the male passengers. The officer continued his little speech by noting that before the Revolution, foreigners always received preferred treatment and were allowed to be first in everything. Now things had changed, he said, and everyone was equal. The word "equal" figured prominently in his remarks, and it was immediately evident that "equal" meant Chinese went first and foreigners waited.

Nancy was now beginning to be really unhappy, and crying quite lustily. Ritchie Davis pushed through the crowd to where the officer was standing. Gesturing toward Nancy, he said that the foreign baby had been out on the barge all afternoon and needed to be put aboard as soon as possible. The foreign baby was in danger of exposure because she was only one week old. He lied of course, but Ritchie was guessing that neither the officer nor any of the other Chinese had ever seen a foreign baby before, and would not be able to judge how old Nancy really might be. There was a bit more exchange, because the officer did not want to back down on his announced boarding priorities, but the Chinese were beginning to look at him rather strangely and Nancy was continuing to cry loudly. Finally, he grudgingly agreed to let Lyn take Nancy on board along with the other women and children, and up the swaying companionway and onto the ship's deck they all went.

A China Story: From Peip'ing to Beijing

When we were again together in our cabin a short time later, we removed Nancy's outer garments and let her kick and wriggle on the berth. The warmth, and the freedom to move her arms and legs, did much to improve her spirits and she was quickly in good humor again. Our own spirits also rose rapidly. The cabin looked so clean and bright, with fresh linen on the bunks, and surroundings so comfortable compared to conditions on the barge. We found it difficult to believe we were actually about to get under way, and that weeks of waiting and uncertainty were finally behind us. By no means could we claim to have been through a major ordeal, but the relief was immense that we had passed through the Customs inspection obstacle race, put the long, uncomfortable river trip behind us, and were finally leaving North China.

The British-flag coastal steamer which we boarded was similar to the one on which I had travelled to Canton. Foreign priorities and ideas of equality again prevailed; the Chinese passengers were in the hold, the foreign passengers in the first class cabins and lounge amidships, and steel bars and armed guards kept the two classes of passenger apart. Our cabins in first class opened onto a lounge where we ate our meals, and where at other times passengers gathered to read, talk, play cards, or do whatever they wanted to pass the time. The ship also boasted a doctor, and shortly after we had begun to settle ourselves we asked a steward to send him to our cabin.

The problem was that when we changed Nancy's diapers we noticed streaks of red in her stool. New and untried parents though we were, we knew that blood in the stool was a danger sign, and the discovery generated a whole new set of worries. The doctor who now knocked on the door was a portly Indian of indeterminate age, clad in black trousers, a white shirt unbuttoned and without a tie, and shod in worn carpet slippers. His appearance did not inspire confidence, but he went right to work. After introducing himself he looked at Nancy, pressed on her stomach a bit, and then carefully examined the diaper and its contents.

This completed, the doctor asked what she had been drinking other than nursing. Our first response was orange juice, which was what we had begun to give her in Peip'ing. But then we stopped and thought a moment, because in T'ientsin there was no orange juice in the apartment and we had given her tomato juice instead. The doctor's eyes lit up at that, and he said he was quite certain the red specks we had found were from the tomato juice, incompletely digested because it was a new liquid for Nancy. We should continue to check for any recurrence, he added, but doubted that would happen. Sighs of relief came from us at this news, a satisfied smile appeared on the face of the doctor, and we parted company happy that fears of serious trouble were unfounded.

The trip from T'ientsin took eight days, and we arrived in Hong Kong on March 29th. Nothing particularly exciting occurred en route, but I recall the food was good and the passage comfortable. For some of the passengers though, all men, the trip became a nightmare. The first day out someone suggested a friendly game of poker to while away the time, and several others quickly picked up on the idea. Lyn thought I might find this fun, but after watching the play for a short while I concluded the game was no place for a new husband and father, particularly one who played poker as poorly as I did and had such meager financial resources. The hunch proved right. As the days passed, the stakes moved higher, and the tension mounted. The game did start as a genial way to pass the time and add a bit of excitement to the trip, but the winners continued to win and the losers to lose. The light-hearted entertainment had become deadly serious by the fifth day. When the game closed at the voyage's end, some of the losers were down by US$2-3,000, more than half my year's salary and far more than some of the losers could afford.

Hong Kong was a transit stop for us, where we put our hold baggage in the hands of forwarding agents and booked passage by air for Shanghai. All the ECA group stayed at the Gloucester House Hotel on Victoria Island, an unusual place in that the rooms and the reception desk were on the top floors of an office building. This was centrally located for shopping and sightseeing, but we did little of that because Nancy was too small to carry around very far or very often. One evening we did arrange for an amah to stay with Nancy while we went with the group to the Parisian Grill. This was a well-known restaurant featuring good steaks and a piano player whose repertoire included lots of Broadway show tunes from the 30s and 40s. A spot like this was, understandably, highly popular among people who had been in China and were looking for a taste of Europe or North America again.

After three days, during which time we dispatched our trunk on its way to the States, we boarded a CNAC flight for Shanghai on April 2nd. In a sense this was like putting our heads in the mouth of the dragon a second time, but we did not expect to stay in Shanghai very long, and again discounted the prospects that anything serious might happen to us.

Shanghai, April 1949

The Shanghai to which we returned was a city in shock. Communist armies were moving rapidly south toward the Yangtse River, fresh from their sweeping victories in North China and Manchuria. Their aim was to position themselves for an attack on Nanking, the Nationalist capital. No one doubted what the outcome would be, or that Shanghai would fall like a ripe fruit when the time came, but nevertheless soldiers bustled about everywhere. Some were put to work building a wooden barrier around the city's perimeter. The raw material for this was telephone poles, originally shipped from the U.S. to reconstruct communication lines throughout China. These were being planted in the ground to create a fortress palisade, not unlike those built on the western Great Plains of the U.S. during the Indian Wars. As a deterrent, the palisade did not look very formidable; cynics alleged it could be pushed over by a team of medium strong water buffalo, but work to complete the fortress still went on daily.

The headquarters for the ECA China operations was in Shanghai, and there we went to deliver the records from our Peip'ing office, file final reports of what had taken place in Peip'ing during the change in government, and await further instructions. In my case, the latter was a notice of termination because my position was abolished; I also received travel orders for our return to the States and a promotion to Foreign Service Staff Officer, Grade 8. Unfortunately, I would not be serving long enough in the new grade to benefit much from the salary increase.

After landing at the Shanghai airport, we were taken to the Park Hotel where we checked in for our final stay in China. This hotel was quite new, across from the Race Course and some distance from the Bund. The rest of our group from Peip'ing went to different hotels, but I met them the following day when we all began the process of winding up matters, writing reports and giving verbal briefings on everything. The next day was also our first wedding anniversary.

Returning to the hotel, Lyn and I arranged to celebrate our first anniversary with a dinner in the hotel's restaurant on the top floor, a place that afforded a panoramic view of the city around us. The hotel was able to provide an amah to stay with Nancy while Lyn and I made our way to the restaurant. With us went a piece of our wedding cake that Beth Shaw had sealed in a tin cookie box, to be opened on this occasion.

The hotel restaurant was a rather grand place, lots of white table linen and sparkling glassware, and a dance floor. There were several parties underway when we arrived, from the looks of things mostly groups of Chinese businessmen, but with a small scattering of foreigners among them. One of these parties was seated near our table, and at some point in the evening a large ice sculpture was wheeled up to them. We had never seen anything like it, ice carved in the shape of birds and an ice basket to hold fruit and bottles of wine. The whole thing seemed so extravagant, so needlessly wasteful, we were astounded. Here, in a country falling apart, in a city under imminent threat, with widespread need and suffering all about, businessmen were giving themselves lavish entertainment as though they were sitting in San Francisco. What could they be celebrating, we wondered, and why did they not have the taste and sensitivity to curb their ostentation in such troubled circumstances?

Our own low-key celebration was a little dampened by the spectacle of the neighboring table, but not too much. We had a great deal to look back on for a first year of marriage, and we marveled that it was possible to pass through so much turmoil with so little ill effect. In fact, here we were celebrating in a luxury hotel, in contrast with the world around us and in a way that epitomized our whole first year. Now we were a family of three. An uncertain future held a whole new range of variables to contend with, and soon we would be in the States with no job, no profession, not knowing where we would live, and hoping we had saved enough to see us through until some of these unknowns were cleared up. All in all, we concluded it had been a terrific year and we would not have traded it for anything.

We handed over our tin of cake to the waiter and asked him to open it and serve it for dessert. He did so, and returned promptly with two lumpy, and obviously moldy, pieces of wedding cake. We sniffed at them, which confirmed their appearance, and sadly pushed them to one side. The seal on the tin had been imperfect, and air had entered to spoil the cake, but we were not about to consider this an omen of some kind. This was just one more of those things that "happen."

A China Story: From Peip'ing to Beijing

The process of winding up the Peip'ing office affairs was not difficult. We did spend a lot of time waiting for people we had to see, but after a few days it became possible to consider taking some time to look around a bit. I learned ECA maintained a guest house in the city of Hangchow, one of China's fabled centers of culture and tradition and not too far from Shanghai. The beauty of Hangchow's surroundings was considered by many to be second to no other city in China. The city was located on a rail line, about 125 miles southwest of Shanghai, and easily reached by that means. Neither Lyn nor I had seen Hangchow. There was time to make a weekend visit if we were willing to take the risk, and the ECA house was available and fully staffed. Pushing our luck, we decided the trip was worth doing.

With Nancy in her traveling basket, and a few clothes in one of our suitcases, we boarded the train for Hangchow on a Friday afternoon. The ECA guest house was waiting for us, and there was even an amah to look after Nancy while we did some sightseeing. Unfortunately, the next day was rainy and gray, considerably dimming the pleasure of walking around Hangchow's famous West Lake. But we persevered and managed to see some of the pagodas that lined the lake, although the rain made walkways slippery and tricky to follow. There was not time to see anything at all of the city, but at least we got a taste of the Hangchow experience. Nancy was well cared for while we traipsed around, and had not minded either the trip down or the stay at the guest house.

On Sunday we boarded the train for the return trip to Shanghai. This took longer than the trip down, with frequent slowdowns and brief unscheduled stops, but we eventually passed through the wooden defense palisade and into Shanghai's North Station. At the ECA office next day I was telling colleagues about our weekend trip, the rain, and the comfortable quarters we had, when one of them interrupted to comment we were lucky to be back. The rail line to Hangchow had been cut the night of our return. Whether service would be restored, given the rapidly deteriorating military situation, was highly uncertain. This was news most chastening. While the line did reopen a while later, we had been very lucky. We had guessed right again, but at that point I swore the time had finally come to stop pushing our luck.

Inflation was by then more dizzying than ever, which seemed impossible because it had been bad for such a long time. Paper currency was bundled in packages of GY$ thousands and then tied together to make up larger packages of GY$ millions. People did not bother to count individual bills, there were just too many of them, but they did count the number of packages of bills. Money was too bulky to carry around in pockets or purses. Strung together, enough money for a few everyday purchases could require a bundle a foot or more in length. We ventured into a candy store located off the lobby of our hotel one day, and selected a pound of chocolates to be paid with a large bunch of bank notes we were openly carrying with us. The shopkeeper smiled ruefully, and placed the money on one side of the scale balance and the candy on the other. The money actually outweighed the candy.

The growing inconvenience of paper currency was forcing other solutions to the problem of conducting business. Silver currency, sometimes called "Mex," circulated freely. These were coins about the size of a silver U.S. dollar, but struck with the profiles of Chinese leaders such as Yuan Shih Kai, first president of China, and Sun Yat Sen, Father of the Republic. As a general rule, two silver coins were worth one U.S. dollar, but the money markets generated exchange rates that differed from this rough equivalency. For example, rates were different for "big heads" and "small heads," referring to the size of the head of the man shown on the coin. For some reason, coins with "little heads" were thought to have more silver than those with "big heads," but the unwary person changing money might not know this. In that case, he might accept two "big head" coins in exchange for his dollar, whereas they would trade for less than two "small heads" when he came to convert them into something else, such as paper currency. Inflation had grown so rapidly by the time we were ready to leave Shanghai there was not enough paper currency in circulation to accommodate transactions. In order to get around this problem, banks were issuing cashier's checks in astronomical amounts, and these in turn were changing hands as currency.

Finally, cashier's checks drawn on U.S. banks, and in U.S. dollars, were also circulating. Because the legitimacy of these checks was doubtful, they exchanged at discounts of 30-40 percent. If someone knew his way around the money exchanges, and was lucky, he could start with Chinese silver dollars (playing the "head" game craftily), move into U.S. paper currency, and then convert to U.S. dollar cashier's checks. In the process, the value of his starting stake (in U.S. dollars) could more than double. On the other hand, he could wind up with worthless paper.

A China Story: From Peip'ing to Beijing

After three weeks all the reporting, accounting and assorted paper work was finished, my usefulness to ECA, and China, at an end. Once again it was time to pack our things and be on our way. We said our goodbyes to the group with whom we travelled from Peip'ing, who would be leaving shortly after us, and were driven to the airport. At ten o'clock on the morning of April 23rd, we boarded the Pan Am flight for Tokyo, Wake Island and Honolulu. The airport was quiet, and there were many empty seats on our plane.

With plenty of space at our feet for Nancy's basket, we settled in comfortably for the first leg of our flight "home," whatever and wherever that might turn out to be. Part of what was passing through our minds, and into our conversation, was relief we were leaving a country about to fall apart. This was mixed with amazement that many more people were not on the same plane. To us, reasons to leave seemed so obvious. Unless you were already a Communist partisan, the future was nothing but fearful uncertainty.

Also, of course, we were taking stock of who we now were, what had become of us, and where we might be heading. Only a bit more than two years had passed since, unknown to each other and disinterested in any romantic association, we had stumbled into an acquaintance in a far-off country, rich in history and bitterly immersed in a cruel civil war. Within that brief time span we had entered a marriage, begat a child, lost our jobs, and weathered, both together and apart, several situations fraught with a potential for serious consequences. We knew we were taking away from China a rare and wonderful experience. Strangely, we also knew this would remain with us in the years ahead and, in ways then hard to imagine, would shape our lives and the lives of our children.

A month later the Shanghai airport was in chaos as people actually fought for places on any outbound flight. The Communists had crossed the Yangtze River on April 20th, three days before our departure, and quickly occupied Nanking. Hardly pausing, their forces then converged on Shanghai, which fell on May 25th.

EPILOGUE

Interim, 1949-1983

The years following our departure brought enormous changes to China, albeit of different scales, different natures and different impacts. The orderly transition from Nationalist to Communist rule we witnessed at the beginning of 1949, the proper and reasonable handling of foreigners that marked those early months, and the possibility that some rapprochement in U.S./Chinese relations might emerge, all began to erode soon after we left. Mutual recognition between the two countries never took place, with the result that news of subsequent developments in China had to come indirectly through refugees and other foreign nationals. U.S. citizens who remained in China after all diplomatic posts had been vacated were at great risk, and many served prison terms before being allowed to leave the country.

After nine years of the new regime, its leader, Mao Tse Tung, pushed China into the "Great Leap Forward." This was a vast program to create communes as the means to do everything, from agriculture and local industry to defense and education, and act as vehicles for decentralization. At the same time, this was also a huge step toward theoretical communism and the destruction of traditional family structures and individualism. By the end of a decade, a myriad of mistakes in conception, organization and execution, plus some natural disasters, had cost the lives of millions, brought stagnation to agriculture and industry, and generated such internal criticism of the whole program that Mao felt compelled to step down as Chairman of the People's Republic.

193

In 1966, a program known as the "Cultural Revolution" was unleashed to radicalize the youth and put pressure on the educational and party bureaucracies. The result was another period of upheaval that struck at a wide range of targets, but chief among them were those with any real or suspected previous connection with wealth, status and education, former "capitalists," art objects from China's cultural heritage, university campuses, and anyone or anything accused of insufficient "redness." Surprisingly, this period also saw a beginning of improved relations with the U.S., starting with a secret visit to China by Secretary of State Henry Kissinger in 1971.

Following Mao's death in 1976 a strong reaction to this cultural chaos brought back to power those who had been driven from it. Now led by Deng Xiaoping, the new leadership officially declared the Cultural Revolution at an end in 1977. Two years later a new era in U.S/China relations began with formal agreements that opened opportunities for economic growth and change at an unprecedented rate. As this took place China shed much of its Soviet-style communist orientation in economic matters in favor of market-oriented policies, but retained tight control over the political sphere via a one-party authoritarian system.

As part of this opening-up process, China began sending small missions made up of different specialists to make contact with counterparts in the U.S. One of the early groups was a team of ping pong players, whose style and competence quickly made headlines everywhere. Another such mission, but one attracting much less attention in the press, was composed of people from the medical professions. This group, scheduled to make visits to Washington D.C. and San Francisco in the Spring of 1973, included Dr. Khati Lim, once again head of obstetrics at the former Peking Union Medical College Hospital.

The State Department invited Lyn to a reception for Dr. Lim and her colleagues in the Watergate Hotel, the guest list for which included mostly State Department wives who had children delivered by Dr. Lim in Peip'ing. Lyn arranged to have our second oldest child included in the invitation because we had named this daughter "Khati," after Dr. Lim. This daughter was, at the time, a pre-med student at Harvard, so the meeting of the two proved a great success. Dr. Lim not only met a namesake, but also met someone who shared the link of being a woman about to enter the field of medicine. For the final stop of the group, in San Francisco, Lyn arranged for Dr. Lim to meet Nancy as well, the child she had helped deliver in Peip'ing twenty-four years earlier.

Beijing, July 1983

The large change in U.S./China relations had now been in effect for more than a decade. Americans were once again visiting China as tourists, though not yet in large numbers. I had been assigned to participate in a World Bank agricultural sector survey mission in Thailand, scheduled to take place during the summer of 1983. Since this would coincide with Lyn's summer vacation, the timing seemed just right for us to take a week's worth of annual leave to visit Beijing en route to Bangkok. The Communists had moved the nation's capital back north and renamed it Beijing, which translates as "northern capital" written in the newly established Pinyin system of transliteration. Through a colleague in the Bank, we arranged a special tour for just the two us, one which provided an interpreter/guide, a car and chauffeur, and freedom to choose our own schedule and go where we wished. While this sometimes coincided with places the guide wanted us to visit, we were surprised to have great leeway in meeting people and looking for places with special meaning for us.

We arrived on time in Beijing at around mid-day, weather warm in the mid-eighties and hazy. The airport was very quiet, almost deserted, with no signs of any other air traffic, either expected or recently arrived. Customs and Immigration procedures went smoothly, and once through them we were greeted by our guide, a smiling young woman in her mid-twenties. While exchanging greetings and talking a bit about what we expected to see in Beijing, we mentioned that we were bearing a letter to Dr. Khati Lim from our daughter Khati, and hoped to be able to see Dr. Lim and deliver it in person. The guide expressed regrets, but had to report that Dr. Lim had died a few days earlier and the newspapers had been filled with stories about her medical achievements ever since.

Though disappointed at this setback to our plans so early in the visit, in no time at all we were on our way into the city in an air-conditioned Toyota. The drive took us along a tree-lined, shaded road that led onto a large thruway, but from that point very little of the city was recognizable to us as we moved along — high-rise apartments, construction everywhere, walls that once defined the city gone, and lots of auto traffic. We had expected something like this, but the scope and pace of change were surprising.

We soon arrived at the Peking Hotel, once a grand old place near the heart of a foreign community consisting, in our day, of the Legation Quarter and Morrison Street (now using its Chinese title of Wangfujing Street). To the west we could see the roofs of the Forbidden City and Tienanmen Square, to the east a barely recognizable Wangfujing Street that still featured shops selling books, prints, ceramics, curios and the like. Before us ran the grand Chang An Boulevard that paralleled the Legation Quarter and the glacis that once protected it.

The hotel wing where we would stay had been re-decorated, with Russian assistance, in a heavy decor reminiscent of the thirties. A new wing, expected to reflect American tastes, was still under construction. Once in our room we found things rather dismal — hospital-styled beds on metal frames, rugs that were faded and none too clean, a bath room with all basics but furnished with fraying towels, ugly lamps, and a television set that functioned quite well. In many ways the surroundings were more or less what we expected, but the hotel had a depressing air to it.

The China we left was a country badly battered by years of war, first with an external enemy, Japan, and later by civil conflict between sides holding vastly different economic and political objectives. What we were about to see was a society dealing with the need to reconstruct, and doing so by making a major economic transformation from old ways. This was probably taking place too rapidly to assess the new ventures against possible alternatives. In the process, whether by the physical changes taking place or deliberate neglect, the new China was also destroying evidence of its once great cultural, intellectual and economic achievements. During the week ahead of us we did not expect to undertake any serious analysis of what was happening in China, but we could compare what we were seeing with what we remembered.

First of all, we wanted to see what had happened to places where we had lived. The famed hut'ungs of Beijing were rapidly disappearing and high-rise buildings of all kinds were replacing them. The guide and chauffeur often did not recognize the name of hut'ungs we wished to visit, and we tried to guide them. This did not always work because compounds in the hut'ungs were hard to recognize by their exterior walls, and we had forgotten old house numbers. The first compound where Lyn had lived was still standing, but it was undergoing major alterations of some kind and Lyn was visibly moved by the disarray she saw in the old place. In what we took to be our first house as a married couple, the current residents were not aware foreigners had ever rented the place, and therefore could not confirm our guess that we had once lived there. Once inside the compounds visited we found several families now living in space we once had to ourselves; often additional shed-like buildings had been put up in what had been courtyards. Though we must have seemed strange to them, the new tenants were all friendly to us, offering babies to be held and inviting us to share cups of tea.

We never located the compound Lyn had shared with Dorie and the Scott sisters, but we did find the old Peking American School, another emotional event for Lyn. The school name and the large lamps by the front door were gone, but we were allowed to enter and look around and found things pretty much as we remembered them. We could not positively identify the Peking Union Church, where we were married, but did find a coal yard/truck garage on a site that could have been the church. The Peking Union Medical Hospital, now called the Capital Hospital, was much as we remembered it from the outside, and visibly busy with patients and visitors.

What we were finding was the start of a makeover of old Peip'ing neighborhoods still functioning much as they did in the days of the Manchu Dynasty. One could well argue the time had long since been reached when more efficient, more hygienic and maybe more comfortable housing should replace them, but the change was removing a large part of what had once made the city so alive and attractive. It saddened us to see this change from traditional compounds, with their opportunities for imaginative diversity in living style, into a metropolis of high-rise housing projects.

Equally important on our list of things to do was to find a few of Lyn's former PAS students, if possible. The parents of some, probably many, had managed to find their way to Taiwan or Hong Kong, and from there a few had found ways to reach the States. Nevertheless, we reasoned many former students must still be living in Beijing and it environs. Our first contact was with Annie, a former student who worked at the Beijing Zoo as part of the team taking care of the pandas there. With her help we tracked down a few others, and arranged for further meetings.

As noted earlier, the Chinese students in PAS all came from well-to-do families, and thus became targets for the persecution and destruction that marked the Cultural Revolution. In the two meetings we had with former students, conducted without the presence of our guide and chauffeur, there was opportunity to hear some of the specifics from that period. We heard accounts of widespread beatings with sticks and harassment from hostile crowds, lengthy periods on communal work farms in the countryside, forced labor in the extensive system of tunnels being dug as part of an air raid protection system, elderly parents forced to pull coal carts and sweep the streets, sudden eviction from family households with only what could be carried. One of the group had spent fifteen years in prison, followed by five more years at a work camp. Although he received a formal apology from the government for the "mistake" that had sent him to prison, and at the time had a teaching job somewhere at the college level, this must have been a very grim experience. Even Dr. Lim, as well known and accomplished as she was, spent time in rural work camps before being restored to key positions in the medical college and its hospital.

Despite the stories we were hearing, people seemed to be bearing up with amazing good humor. There was much talk of other students and teachers, and where they might be now, and the mood in the group was warm and positive. The hostess for one occasion felt lucky to be living in the servant quarters of her former family home. There was talk about scarcities of things, and the under-the-counter ways of dealing with them. Everyone agreed that good contacts at a high government/party level were necessary to get good housing, or access to university places. These and similar references seemed to indicate that the new China was showing traits that had been prevalent under the displaced old regime. Recalling Dr. Lim's comments at the time when the Communists were about to capture Peip'ing, she thought the new regime might mean two steps forward and one step back. Indeed, this was the way things seemed to be moving under China's new leadership.

On the streets, in stores and restaurants, at locations picked by our guide, we encountered more situations where different forces seemed at work. Service in the hotel was diffident, and old hands in the dining room went to the sideboards to refill cups of tea rather than ask for a waiter; clerks in stores selling souvenirs seemed to make little effort to attract sales; in general, service in government establishments of all kinds tended to be lethargic.

In contrast, there seemed increasing signs of individual efforts to do business of some kind. Driving out to the Ming Tombs we saw many farmers spreading wheat on the road so that cars passing over would thresh it. Our guide volunteered the view that farmers were now all so rich they have more bicycles and other consumables than city dwellers can afford. Numerous petty street merchants were selling clothing, appliances, and varied food items, fresh and processed. Here and there we found artisans selling hand-made household utensils, in one case a man making small Chinese opera figurines from bits of painted dough. There was a "free market" near the Temple of Heaven which also included a produce section, and just outside were many curb-side stands, also selling vegetables and fruit.

As we again boarded a plane to carry us away from China, it appeared to us the country was emerging from some very harsh times and moving rapidly toward higher standards of living for many. We did not reach any conclusions about change in political matters because it seemed unwise to explore this area. Suffice it to say the China we knew from our first stay was not known for its concern with civil rights matters, and the new regime seemed unlikely to bring changes in personal freedoms that were any improvement.

To complete this story of our nuclear family's beginnings, some reference to how this China experience affected the years that followed seems appropriate. My awakening to the devastating effects of war, and not just in China and Japan, along with the experience of working for CRM and ECA, left me with a strong desire to have some role in the economic reconstruction effort so clearly required world-wide. To do this required more education, i.e., I needed a profession before anyone would want to hire me for a decent job in the field of economic development. Soon after our return to the States, and an unproductive job search among U.S. government agencies, I enrolled in a graduate economics program at Columbia University in the summer of 1949. Three years later, thanks to a great financial boost from both (a) the GI Bill, and (b) the availability of public housing on a former military base near New York City, I had met all the requirements for a doctorate save the thesis. Our family had meanwhile grown to three daughters, and in the late summer of 1952 we set off for a life in academia.

James B. Hendry

Over the next fourteen years we would spend five of them living abroad while I took part in two university technical assistance projects. The first of these was in Viet Nam with the Michigan State University Group, from which came a book, "The Small World of Khanh Hau," which analyzed the economy of a small delta village. The second was with the Harvard Advisory Group in East Pakistan, a region now known as Bangladesh. My role there was as advisor on agricultural sector planning for the Provincial Government.

At both these overseas postings, Lyn resumed her teaching at American Schools, and in the latter case also acted as Head Mistress of the Dacca American School. In the course of living abroad, and traveling to and from the overseas postings, our daughters saw much of the world very early in their growing-up years. Their perspective on matters international became quite different from their contemporaries, as reflected partly in a comment one made after a day at school back in the States: "Those dumb kids in the second grade don't even know where Bangkok is!"

Based on the experience gained in the overseas assignments, the World Bank recruited me in 1966 to serve as economist in their agriculture lending programs in developing countries. This association lasted until mandatory retirement from the Bank in 1986, during which time I worked mainly with countries in North Africa, Sub-Saharan Africa, and South Asia.

Lyn's excellence in teaching brought her an Honorary Doctorate of Humane Letters from Georgetown University in 1979. The degree recognized her achievements in the field of secondary school education, and cited her "impressive experience" in both the U.S. and various schools abroad, e.g., Peip'ing, Saigon and Dacca. The degree also took particular notice that the courses she taught were in Economics, History of the Far East, and Advanced Placement European History.

Our family's early experience abroad seems to have played some role in our daughters' future activities as well. One served in the Peace Corps, first as a volunteer and later as General Counsel, and also as attorney for an international association of women judges; another spent a large part of a medical career providing care for indigent immigrants (Latino and Asian); and a third taught at an elementary school in Guam.

A China Story: From Peip'ing to Beijing

Thus ends the story of one family's beginnings in China. The purpose was to provide a bit of perspective on both a major event in China's long history, and how what happened at that time related to lives and careers that followed. To future family members this will be a source of family history; for others, may it prove a good read about a fascinating period in a once exotic part of the world.

Made in the USA
Las Vegas, NV
16 September 2024

95355474R00118